Church Authority
in American Culture

Church Authority in American Culture

The Second Cardinal Bernardin Conference

●

—Catholic Common Ground Initiative—

Introduction by Philip J. Murnion

A Herder & Herder Book
The Crossroad Publishing Company
New York

The Crossroad Publishing Company
370 Lexington Avenue, New York, NY 10017

Printed in the United States of America

Library of Congress Cataloging-in-Publication Data

Cardinal Bernardin Conference (2nd : 1998 : Oconomowoc, Wis.)
    Church authority in American culture : the second Cardinal
Bernardin Conference / Catholic Common Ground Initiative :
introduction by Philip J. Murnion.
      p.   cm.
    "A Herder & Herder book."
    Includes bibliographical references.
    ISBN 0-8245-1788-1 (pbk.)
    1. Church—Authority—History of doctrines—20th century—
Congresses.   2. Christianity and culture—United States—
History—20th century—Congresses.   3. Catholic Church—United
States—History—20th century.   I. Catholic Common Ground
Initiative   II. Title.
BX1746.C275   1998
262'.8'08822—dc21
                                        99-11107
                                           CIP

1 2 3 4 5 6 7 8 9 10 03 02 01 00 99

Contents

Abbreviations

Documents of Vatican II

AA — *Apostolicam Actuositatem* (Decree on the Apostolate of the Laity)

CD — *Christus dominus* (Decree on the Pastoral Office of Bishops in the Church)

DH — *Dignitatis humanae* (Declaration on Religious Liberty)

GS — *Gaudium et spes* (Pastoral Constitution on the Church in the Modern World)

LG — *Lumen gentium* (Dogmatic Constitution on the Church)

SC — *Sacrosanctum concilium* (Constitution on the Sacred Liturgy)

Papal Documents

CA — *Centesimus annus* (John Paul II, encyclical, May 1, 1991)

HG — *Humani generis* (Pius XII, encyclical, 1950)

HV — *Humanae vitae* (Paul VI, encyclical, July 25, 1968)

MD — *Mulieris dignitatem* (John Paul II, apostolic letter, August 15, 1988)

MI — *Maximum illud* (Benedict XV, encyclical, 1919)

OS — *Ordinatio sacerdotalis* (John Paul II, apostolic letter, May 22, 1984)

National Council of Catholic Bishops

CP — *The Challenge of Peace: God's Promise and Our Response*, May 3, 1983.

EJ   *Economic Justice for All: Pastoral Letter on*
            Catholic Social Teaching and the U.S. Economy,
            November 18, 1986.

Other Church Documents
AAS   *Acta Apostolicae Sedis*

INTRODUCTION

Philip J. Murnion

Among the pastor subscribers to *CHURCH,* the National Pastoral Life Center quarterly for parish ministry, the most popular cover art has been Ford Maddox Brown's very realistic portrayal, "Jesus Washing Peter's Feet." The pastors see this as the model for their ministry, the exemplar for their exercise of leadership and authority. It expresses graphically what has come to be called the servant model of leadership or authority. I say "leadership or authority" as if the two were one, because one other feature in the current understanding of authority is that it is an exercise of leadership, fostering rather than coercing acceptance of the demands of discipleship. Implicit in this conflation of authority, leadership, and servanthood, at its best, is the expectation that the community of the church will not be a place where " the rulers lord it over them and their great ones make their authority over them felt." No, it should not be like that in the church. "Rather whoever wishes to be great among you will be your servant; whoever wishes to be first among you will be the slave of all." Thus the subscript to the pope's signature, *servus servorum Dei* (servant of the servants of God).

At the same time, the servant model of authority can appeal to another strain in culture and church, namely, an egalitarian temper and the desire to overcome widespread suspicion of all those in institutional roles of authority. The tendency is then to bracket other scenes in the gospels in which Jesus "speaks as one with authority," as where he "scatters the proud in the conceit of their hearts" by challenging whoever is sinless to cast the first stone. Or when Jesus reprimands Peter's desire for political revolution. Or when Jesus commands the apostles to do what they are told, even when they do not understand, as in distributing food to the hungry crowd or letting down their nets for a catch. Or Jesus' announcement that he has come not "to establish peace on earth" but "rather division."

Jesus' model for authority is not simple. In fact, the proper exercise of authority will always be a delicate balance between command and compassion, sanctions and sympathy, insistence on adherence to community norms and respect for the conscience of the individual. There is always the challenge of locating where authority lies, how far it extends, and how it must be exercised. It is not surprising, then, that the issue of authority in the church has come to the fore as the church struggles to understand the full meaning of Vatican II's reordering of relationships in and of the church. And this in a culture that, as Philip Selznick says in the following pages, is suffering "the erosion of parental, religious, and political authority."

CATHOLIC COMMON GROUND AND AUTHORITY

The Catholic Common Ground Initiative was established by the late Cardinal Joseph Bernardin to foster dialogue regarding critical issues facing the church. His concern was that widening polarization between "camps" in the church was hindering the church's capacity to address these issues. The question of authority was important in both the establishment of the Catholic Common Ground Initiative and reactions to it. Among the issues identified in the Initiative's founding paper, *Called to Be Catholic*, were the gap between church teaching and the convictions of many Catholics; the manner of decision-making and consultation in the church; the responsibility of theology to authoritative church teaching; the place of collegiality and subsidiarity in the relations between Rome and the American episcopacy. Implicit in other issues as well, such as religious education, the respective roles of laity and clergy, the role of women, lie concerns about authority—authoritative church teaching and access to positions of authority in the church. On the other hand, many of those who opposed the Initiative's call for dialogue saw it as a weakening of church authority and an encouragement of dissent.

It seemed quite appropriate to the committee for the Initiative, therefore, to devote the second Cardinal Bernardin Catholic Common Ground Conference to the subject of church authority in American culture. The plan for the conference entailed inviting a panel of four experts to prepare papers on aspects of the question and to solicit reactions to these papers in advance of the conference from those who would participate. Participants were to include members of the Initiative committee and guests invited to represent different positions and viewpoints in the church, particularly regarding the exercise of authority. The format of the conference itself engaged the authors of the papers in mutual critique and all of the participants in discussion both with the authors and among themselves. In the exchanges among the panelists they were each asked to offer a resume of their paper and indicate what others might regard as a weakness in their position. Then each was offered a critique by the others and had an opportunity to respond. Open discussion with all the participants followed. This volume contains the original papers and a record of the discussions with the panelists.

FRAMING THE DISCUSSION

The panelists were chosen to represent and to reflect on different levels in the church. The Reverend Avery Dulles, S.J., was asked to reflect on the exercise of papal authority; Reverend Joseph Komonchak on the teaching and authority of episcopal conferences; and Reverend James Coriden on the exercise of local pastoral authority. Finally, Dr. Philip Selznick was asked for his reflections on authority in American society.

Father Dulles went to the heart of present discussions about papal authority by reviewing the teaching on artificial contraception in *Humanae vitae* and on ordination of women in *Ordinatio sacerdotalis*. He identified ways in which the exercise of teaching in the two instances were similar, underscored what he saw to be the proper exercise of papal authority, and distinguished what he described as the "sacral" context of the teaching and what he saw to be the "secular" context of the criticisms of the two documents.

Father Komonchak reflected on the major pastoral letters by the American bishops on peace and the economy and the role of episcopal conferences in the collegial exercise of authority. He went beyond this, however, to consider the conditions for effective exercise of authority, drawing on both theological and sociological theories of authority. His concern was shared by Professor Selznick, whose view is that "most questioning of authority has to do with the way it is exercised, not with the initial grant or premise." Father Komonchak agreed further with Dr. Selznick that authority lies in the community, not just or even primarily in certain persons or offices.

Father Coriden presented three "case studies" regarding discipline, not doctrine: the use of general absolution in parishes, the "good-faith solution" where marriages cannot be annulled through the normal canonical procedures, and the availability of due process to resolve a conflict between a pastor and a staff. The three cases were meant to support both the room for "pastoral accommodation" and the right and opportunity for those in the local church to exercise discernment about what is best and in keeping with the Gospel. He completed his reflection with a list of characteristics of authority identified in the scriptures. If there is a shortcoming in his position, he acknowledged, it might be in his overly optimistic view of human nature.

Professor Selznick, who was invited because of his stature in American social science rather than his specific knowledge of the church, addressed not only the dissipation of authority in American culture but also conditions for the exercise of authority in civil society. He distinguished between authoritarian regimes and authoritative order, the latter "a system governed by widespread respect—among the rulers and the ruled—for shared values, purposes, and institutions, including institutions that represent legitimate authority." He judged that in American culture "a radical relativism has taken hold," with the result that "the very idea of truth—especially moral truth—is challenged." In response to this situation he suggested that the two poles to be avoided are a kind of terminal uncertainty on the one hand and the effort to "escape uncertainty by embracing rigid and unchangeable conceptions of rights, duties, and authority."

Many Aspects and Levels of the Question

The goal of the conference, and the goal of the Catholic Common Ground Initiative in general, is to foster among people with significantly differing positions the kind of dialogue that will make it possible to identify more clearly just where the differences lie and, if possible, to widen the ground of agreement so as to enrich the wider church's treatment of the issue at hand. It must be said at the outset that the conference had only very modest success in this aim. While the original plan for the conference called for articulating propositions on which the participants could agree, it became clear that the time and the process did not make this possible. The participants largely agreed that the opportunity to gather in prayer, the celebration of the Eucharist, and personal contact did help both to clarify many aspects of the question of authority (and indeed of broader questions of ecclesiology) and to bring about an appreciation of their shared faith and good will. At times, however, the process itself got in the way of pursuing areas of contention and people's unfamiliarity with one another required more time to create the grounds for trust and candor necessary for the true dialogue.

Rather than achieve a joint statement, the participants left to the organizers the responsibility to offer a record and reflection of the discussion. We believe that the record contained here—the papers themselves and the discussion—does provide a rich treasure of reflection on a central question in the church. Nonetheless, it may be useful to offer one set of observations on the levels and aspects of the issue that emerged in the conference.

THE LOCATION OF AUTHORITY IN THE CHURCH

One obvious question is the location of authority in the church: who exercises authority, who shares in the exercise of authority? There was no doubt among the participants that Christ endowed the church with authority. Neither was there doubt that the pope and bishops, as successors of the apostles, are particularly endowed with the responsibility and guidance of the Spirit to teach authoritatively and to govern the church for the sake of fidelity to the tradition. It was not so clear how the bishops share in that authority, individually or as a conference of bishops, how theologians participate in the development of teaching, or how local pastors have the authority to adapt to local conditions and need (for example, in Father Coriden's cases of general absolution or the good-faith solution to marriage cases). Of greatest importance to some, for theological reasons or even because of the state of contemporary culture, is the authority of the pope. For others, perhaps for the same reasons, it is the sharing of authority from the conscience of the individual, the judgment of the local pastor, to the conclusions of the conferences of bishops.

More deeply at stake is the question of how revelation has been entrusted to the church and how the Holy Spirit guides the church in its reception and understanding of the message of Jesus. One view stresses the communication of revelation and the Spirit to the whole church, pointing especially to the documents of Vatican II as grounds for this view. Another view locates revelation and guidance of the Spirit in and through the apostles and their bishop successors, and especially in the ministry of the successor of St. Peter, the bishop of Rome. If one holds to the former view, then consultation in the church prior to teaching is a requirement to discern the truth. If the latter, consultation can be helpful but is not essential, and for particular situations the *Nota Praevia* that Paul VI appended to the council's *Dogmatic Constitution on the Church* gives the pope the right to act on his own rather than collegially. As Father Dulles argues, "The plenitude of power is vested in a single body" that has the final responsibility "to discern the presence of the Spirit" in initiatives that arise in the church. Implied are quite different views of the significance of Vatican II. Did it mark what some have called a "paradigm shift" in ecclesiology and in understanding the location of revelation and authority in the church, or was it "more a nuancing of what had been previously taught," in Father Dulles's words. At issue, then, is whether consultation and engagement of the whole church, and especially of the college of bishops, are required for authentic exercise of authority or for effective exercise of authority. Indeed, what is the relationship between authentic and effective exercise of authority?

Once one explores the difference between authentic and effective exercise of authority, one is deciding on a particular definition of authority. Professor Selznick offered this definition: "Authority is a rightful claim to deference or obedience." Some would suggest that authority involves more than the rightful claim; it is distinguished from the exercise of power over others by the acceptance of its claim to deference or obedience. Indeed, the panel and other discussants agreed on the need for trust as the basis for the exercise of authority. In this respect Father Dulles lamented the culture of suspicion that undermines authority in the church. Father Komonchak found helpful Cardinal Newman's expression of "the ecclesial conditions within which authority exists and which are required for it to be acknowledge and respected: 'admiration, trust, and love' for Christ and the church." Father Coriden stressed the importance of respect and trust for the local church and the members of the church as well as their trust in the hierarchy. To what extent, then, do conditions for effectiveness affect claims of authenticity?

A condition for the exercise and reception of authority stressed by Father Komonchak seemed important to the discussion, namely, the need for conversion. While the writing of Bernard Lonergan was not directly alluded to, one could infer from many remarks the importance of the kind of intellectual (overcoming of bias), moral (commitment to values), and religious (experience of God's love) conversion needed to exercise and accept the authority of the Gospel and of the church. Archbishop Weakland spoke of his experience visiting monasteries as abbot primate of the Benedictines, when it would become clear in his consultations which monks offered the most useful reflections because of their evident wisdom of mind and life. They were the *pars sanior* in the community, those faithful in observance who had the good of the community at heart. Father Dulles spoke of the need for people to be steeped in the tradition if they are to offer helpful consultation. Others lamented that the poor state of people's knowledge of the faith hinders both their own development and their involvement in dialogue in the church. Still others talked of ways that the culture adversely affects efforts to live and articulate the truth of the Gospel and the demands of discipleship. In short, what we know, what we value, and how much our approach to the life of the church arises from faith as an experience of God's love deeply affect how we enter into dialogue.

Dr. Ann Lin addressed the same question when she cited the experience of God as foundational for the church and for the exercise of authority in the church. If people have an experience of God in a community of worship, she points out, then they can come to realize that "it is not just your heart that gets carried away by the singing, but your head and the intellect . . . that get engaged by this God, too." Her appeals for church leaders both to provide opportunities for people to experience God's presence and to respect and build on people's experience of God in the community of the church found an echo in the comment by many that the teaching that is most important in the church is preaching, the appeal to faith, of faith speaking to faith, of faith leading to action.

Church and Culture

The relationship between the church and culture was at issue in many ways. Dr. R. Scott Appleby and Dr. Ann Lin were particularly concerned about the fact that younger generations simply did not start from the same place regarding the question of authority. Dr. Appleby pointed out how much younger people grant their own experience primacy over claims of authority. He finds in them something akin to the assumption of "immediate contact with the divine that is not mediated by the tradition or by church authority." For these people, authority must offer not just any reasons for the positions it takes but reasons that relate directly to people's experience. The desire for reasons behind church teaching and discipline is not restricted to younger generations, participants agreed, even if at some basic level faith always exceeds reason. It may be, as Father Komonchak asserted, that the reason offered for a particular teaching is simply that it has always been part of the tradition. It was Michael Novak's view that the church "community, more than any religious community in the world, gives reasons. We believe in giving reasons."

A different take on culture and reasons was expressed by other participants like Judge John Noonan and Father Komonchak. Judge Noonan argued that the record of history is replete with instances where what was definitive teaching underwent change precisely under the influence of culture. He and Father Dulles engaged in the sharpest dispute of the conference, one that could well have been pursued further, regarding religious liberty. Judge Noonan cited the council's declaration of religious liberty as a correction of earlier teaching, while Father Dulles was convinced that this did not correct any prior teaching.

Consultation and culture came together as well in the discussion of the *sensus fidelium* (sense of the faithful). Father Imbelli suggested that Father Dulles's view evidences a certain "wariness in appeal to *sensus fidelium.*" That wariness seemed to be prevalent in the participants, though in differing degrees and with differing consequences. Consultation with the sense of the faithful, of those who are indeed trying to be faithful, requires care. It cannot be reduced to polling—as useful as this can be. Further, as Father James Heft pointed out, it is of great importance to consult the saints—indeed, those with the kind of maturity in holiness that Archbishop Weakland honored among his monks. Nonetheless, the difficulties entailed cannot eliminate the need to consult the faithful. Furthermore, consultation with the faithful, as Gerald Shea pointed out, is necessary not just for reactions to the inspirations of the hierarchy but for the leadership of the church to be open to the laity's experience of life, to the questions and concerns of people trying to work out their existence in the world. Many cited the U.S. bishops' consultation in preparing the pastoral letters on peace and the economy as outstanding examples of consulting the faithful (and, it might be added, of consulting other wisdom in the culture).

Discussion of these pastoral letters raised another question that links consultation with collegiality and the role of the episcopal conferences. Father Bryan Hehir pointed to what he sees as different modes or criteria for teaching. He asserted that "increasing specificity [in the teaching] means declining authority," meaning that the more specific the bishops were in judging certain actions on issues of economic justice and just defense to be moral or immoral, the less authority they could assert for these positions. At the same time he opined that the bishops could not be so modest when they address bioethical questions and leave to individual consciences the right to make the final judgment. While rehearsing an old dispute between himself and Father Dulles regarding the prudence of bishops offering specific directions in economic and social questions, Father Hehir's main point was rather the question of whether there is a different moral methodology governing the treatment of bioethical questions than economic and other social questions. In short, the question is not just the source of authority but the scope of authority: how specific and in what areas shall the authority be exercised regarding personal and social questions?

To return to the point that authority lies in the community, not just or even primarily in certain persons or offices, building up the community of faith, a community united in faith and prayer, in sacrament and service, is the condition for the exercise of authority. Authority, like community, is not an abstraction but the actual relationships among the people of the church.

FINDING AND BROADENING COMMON GROUND

The hope of the Catholic Common Ground Initiative is to engage people with different, and perhaps polarized, viewpoints in examination of an issue so as to clarify where there is common ground and where there remain differences of conviction and to acquire a better understanding of the nature of these differences, all within the context of the teaching of the church. There are explicit or implicit in the presentations and discussions at the conference some obvious areas of agreement and some clear areas of disagreement. The participants in the conference did not think that there had been sufficient time or discussion to determine just where these areas of agreement and disagreement lay. Yet many of these areas of agreement or disagreement are evident from the text that follows, and my comments may help to illuminate some of these.

Commitment to the authority of Jesus handed on to the church through the Holy Spirit and in a particular way to the apostles and their successors, the bishops, who have the primary responsibility in union with the bishop of Rome for assuring the unity of faith and church, was unquestioned in the group. Also accepted was the need for trust as a condition for the exercise of authority, trust based on shared faith and deepened through shared prayer. For some, increase in trust requires more pervasive readiness among the members of the church to approach official church teaching with deference. For others, it calls for more readiness on the part of those in authority to consult, to provide plausible reasons for their exercise of authority, and for greater acknowledgment of others' share in authority for formulating and determining church doctrine and discipline. (Since the conference, Pope John Paul II has issued the apostolic letter *Apostolos suos,* defining the role of episcopal conferences, their responsibilities, the conditions and scope of their teaching, and the limitations on their teaching authority. While sharpening the distinctions, the letter's implications for the United States remain to be studied.) What is obvious is that the differences are not just strategic but theological, not just a matter of what is most prudent but what is required for the exercise of authority. For all, the deepening of faith and order in the church calls for continual conversion and formation in the community of the church. For all, as well, authority is meant to be a service for building up the community of the church, for bringing the life and message of Jesus to the world, for the salvation of the world.

Trust is also required in the effort to seek common ground, a kind of trust that is not easily achieved in a few days among strangers. Celebrated and of fundamental importance to the participants was their union in Christ, in word and sacrament, in faith and prayer, in community and fellowship. Indeed, one of the results of such a gathering is, as many participants noted, that it challenges the stereotypes one can develop regarding those with whom we disagree. It is easy to be harsh in judging others whom we don't know; one is more ready to acknowledge good faith, good will, and common identity as committed members of the same church when we meet face to face and share the same Eucharist. In other words, in the deepest of essentials, this group was in communion. Yet in facing the future, continuing dialogue is urgent, whether for prudence or fidelity, in trying to discern where the Spirit is leading the church.

1

Humanae Vitae and *Ordinatio Sacerdotalis*

Problems of Reception

Avery Dulles, S.J.

W hen I was asked to discuss one or two sample cases of reception and nonreception of the teaching of the magisterium on the universal level (that is, that of the pope or the college of bishops), I immediately thought of two cases that in our time have provoked clamorous dissent—Paul VI's encyclical *Humanae vitae* (1968) and John Paul II's apostolic letter *Ordinatio sacerdotalis* (1995). A brief account of the one or the other would probably contain nothing new, since the facts are relatively well known and, in their main lines, undisputed. But it occurred to me that it might be instructive to reflect on the analogies between the two cases. The comparison may direct our attention beyond the specific issues raised in each case and throw light on the ways that the magisterium functions, and might function, in the church and the world of our day.

In each of these two cases the pope decided a burning and divisive issue by an authoritative pronouncement that was intended to bring closure to the debate. And in each case a large number of Catholics, especially in Western Europe and North America, vociferously dissented and claimed the right to do so as loyal members of the church. The questions raised by the two cases, while not identical, are in many respects similar. To illustrate the similarities ten sets of considerations may here be mentioned.

Points of Comparison

1. *Biblical Basis*. The direct biblical arguments against contraception, taken mostly from the Old Testament (notably the Onan story of Genesis 38:8–10), were weak and unconvincing. The biblical case against the ordination of women to the priesthood was admittedly stronger, but not so strong that the issue could be definitively settled by the biblical evidence alone. In both cases, therefore, it could be asked: should the relative openness of the biblical teaching be grounds for keeping the question doctrinally open? If "scripture alone" were the criterion, an affirmative answer would be in order. But the Catholic Church, of course, reads scripture in the light of natural law and tradition. It does not subscribe to the Protestant principle of *sola scriptura* (scripture alone).

2. *Tradition*. In each of the two cases the argument from tradition was strong. Popes, bishops, and Catholic theologians who addressed the question down through the centuries were unanimous, at least until the middle of our own century. In the case of contraception the tradition based itself primarily on natural law, whereas in the case of ordination the appeal was primarily to the conduct of Christ and the apostles in establishing and transmitting the priestly office. In both cases the popes of our day (Paul VI and John Paul II) reaffirmed the tradition, calling attention to previous statements of the magisterium.

3. *Ecumenical Considerations.* The Catholic teaching on both issues agrees with that of most Protestant and Anglican communities until the present century, and with the ancient and current teaching of the Orthodox. Since about 1930 however, a substantial number of Anglican and Protestant churches have permitted contraception, at least in certain difficult situations. Since about 1950, the same churches have to an increasing extent admitted women to ecclesiastical orders, including, most recently, the episcopate. No such break with the tradition has occurred in the teaching and practice of the Orthodox churches, which on both issues seem to stand in solidarity with Rome.

4. *The Tradition Impugned.* The arguments from tradition in both instances have been assailed as unsound by some contemporary authors. In the case of contraception it is argued that the tradition was unduly influenced by the Stoic view of nature and by Augustine's negative evaluation of sexual intercourse—a carryover (it is said) from his Manichaean days. In the case of women's ordination the false assumption of female inferiority is frequently alleged to have been the real reason for excluding women from priestly orders. In both cases, therefore, the Christian tradition is held to have been contaminated by alien influences, and in particular by Greek dualism and androcentrism. Those who accept the papal teaching maintain that the respective traditions do not depend upon these extrinsic influences but, as mentioned above, on natural law (in the one case) and on the deliberate choice of Jesus and the apostles (in the other).

5. *Novel Factors.* In both cases new factors have been adduced as reasons supporting a change in doctrine. With regard to contraception some mention the emergence of a more positive view of sexuality, which is seen in our day as positively sustaining the mutual love of spouses even when it is not directed to procreation. In the early 1960s a number of theologians maintained that the invention of anovulant pills permitted a new application of the accepted principle that intercourse

during "safe periods" was legitimate. Others argued that in view of the contemporary population explosion the traditional argument against birth control as preventing the human race from multiplying and filling the earth (cf. Gn 1:28) had lost its validity. The good of the human race today, according to the revisionists, demands the restriction, not the increase, of fertility. Defenders of the tradition replied that the separation of the unitive from the procreative aspects of the marriage act was a violation of the divine plan, that it deprived the act of its true meaning, and that it opened the way to all kinds of perversion.

In the case of women's ordination, advocates of change called attention to the growing prominence of women in positions of power and responsibility. Once women had access on a par with men to all areas of education and professional life, it seemed anachronistic to exclude them from leadership positions in the church, which were de facto (by fact), and even (it would seem) de iure (by law), reserved to the clergy. Putting this argument in more theological terms, some alluded to the accession of women to new roles as a "sign of the times" through which God was sending a message to the church. Opponents of women's ordination, however, replied that the sacramental significance of priesthood, understood in the light of Christ's bridal relationship to the church, demanded that priestly orders be reserved to men alone.

6. *The Process of Decision.* The two cases are similar insofar as the decisive pronouncement was made neither by collegiate action of the bishops nor by the pope speaking *ex cathedra* (by virtue of his office), but by an exercise of the ordinary papal magisterium.

The birth-control question was withdrawn from the Second Vatican Council, presumably because Pope John XXIII and Pope Paul VI regarded it as too technical, too divisive, and too explosive for general discussion. Instead, they appointed a special commission of experts, which was to submit its findings to a supervising commission of cardinals and bishops. Paul

VI went against the overwhelming majority of his fifty-five-person commission of theologians, demographers, and canonists (which included many laypersons) and apparently against a slim plurality of the supervising commission. (Different authors give different tabulations of the final vote, which was never made public.) Did his conduct violate the norms appropriate for the consultative process? Or did he, as pope, have the duty to exercise his own discretion and follow the advice of those whose arguments he found most cogent?

In the case of the ordination of women there was no advisory commission. Vatican II was silent on the issue, apparently because it simply did not come up for discussion. The Congregation for the Doctrine of the Faith in 1976 produced a declaration, approved by Paul VI, to the effect that the church did not see itself as authorized to ordain women to the priesthood. The *Catechism of the Catholic Church*, which had been submitted in draft form to all the bishops in the Catholic Church for their comments, took the position that women could never be admitted to the sacrament of holy orders. Before issuing *Ordinatio sacerdotalis* John Paul II summoned the heads of the episcopal conferences to Rome for a brief consultation, but no report of that meeting was made public. As in the case of *Humanae vitae*, the question is asked: Did the pope rely too much on his own personal views, taking insufficient cognizance of recent ecumenical and theological developments? Should he have commissioned a broader consultation that would take account of new theological perspectives and of the experience of the Protestant and Anglican churches? Or would a broader and more protracted consultation have raised unrealistic expectations?

7. *Primacy and Collegiality*. Vatican II, as already noted, said nothing specific about the use of contraceptives or about the access of women to the ministerial priesthood. While it did assert that the college of bishops, with and under the pope as its head, holds supreme governing and teaching authority, it also asserted that the Roman pontiff has full, supreme, and

universal power in the church and can always exercise that power freely (*LG* 22, 25). It taught expressly that the doctrinal pronouncements of the pope, even when he is not speaking *ex cathedra*, are to be accepted with religious submission of will and mind, according to the manifest intention of the pope (*LG* 25).

The teaching of the council on primacy and collegiality was clarified by the prefatory note of explanation that was appended to *Lumen gentium* by order of the pope himself. This note emphasized the right of the pope to reserve doctrinal questions to himself when he judges fit. He is charged with the responsibility of deciding whether it is more desirable to act personally or collegially in the particular case.

Even if it is granted that the popes did not violate the prescriptions of Vatican II, it can still be debated whether or not they were correct in judging that the two issues we are considering ought to be decided by the pope himself rather than by the united action of the whole episcopate. If it were granted that the popes' procedures were deficient, what effect, if any, would that deficiency have on the binding force of the teachings in question?

8. *Response of the Episcopate*. In the case of *Humanae vitae* the bishops' conferences responded variously and in some cases awkwardly, either making allowance for legitimate dissent or interpreting the encyclical in ways that appeared to blunt the clarity of its teaching. Some said, for example, that in certain circumstances a married couple might be faced by a conflict of duties that would justify the use of contraception. The pope was wounded by the mixed response, but he accepted it in good grace.

In the case of *Ordinatio sacerdotalis* the conferences were generally silent, though a number of prominent bishops, including the presidents of some conferences, expressed their support. In countries such as our own the support given by some bishops was interpreted as perfunctory, while the silence of the others gave the impression that they were seeking to avoid confrontation on an obviously unpopular issue. Even if they agreed, they seemed eager to let Rome take the heat. It is a moot question whether the dissent would have been reduced if the bishops had taken stronger positions in support of the pope.

9. *Public Opinion.* The general public, even within the Catholic Church, was not persuaded by the official declarations on either birth control or female priesthood. If anything, the proportion who opposed the papal position in countries such as the United States grew larger. Did this indicate that the papal teaching was contrary to the *sensus fidelium* (sense of the faithful) and might for that reason be suspected of error? Or did it, on the contrary, show that public opinion in the church can fail to reflect an authentic sense of the faith? Calling attention to the general state of opinion and the impact of the secular journalism, theologians judge that the secular mentality, rather than a specifically Christian rationale, lies at the root of the existing dissent. If so, the *sensus fidelium* could not legitimately be invoked against the papal teaching.

10. *Theological Dissent.* After the appearance of *Humanae vitae* a large number of theologians sought to protect and promote dissenting positions by drawing up open letters and referendums to the effect that the question was still doctrinally open or even that the pope's teaching was erroneous. A few theology professors who vocally opposed Pope Paul's encyclical were dismissed, but most of the dissenters were allowed to keep their positions or, after dismissal, were reinstated without recantation. In the case of *Ordinatio sacerdotalis* prominent theologians and theological societies placed themselves on record as rejecting the pope's position or at least as holding that the papal pronouncement did not settle the issue. Some Catholic periodicals published a stream of articles criticizing the arguments and conclusions of the Holy See. The continuing vocal protests have undoubtedly hindered the development of any consensus among Catholics in favor of the official teaching of their church.

Divergence and Common Ground

The parallelism between the two cases indicates to my mind that the divisions of opinion transcend the particularities of each case. The positions taken on the substantive questions reflect a mentality that potentially extends to an indefinite number of cases. The basic question is whether to accept the longstanding Catholic tradition, authoritatively confirmed by the ecclesiastical teaching office and by the pope as its supreme exponent, or to maintain a critical distance from the tradition and the magisterium and give greater weight to new perspectives that enjoy greater support in society at large. Stated somewhat too crudely, the division is between conservatives and progressives or between the sacral and the secular spirit. Since the two sides follow different principles, neither side finds the arguments of the other persuasive.

In spite of the ideological cleft, it is possible for reasonable adherents of each side to appreciate their adversaries' point of view. Few conservatives are so extreme that they deny all mutability in the tradition or question the possibility that the church might have something to learn from developments in secular society. The church itself encourages its members to be men and women of their own time and to proclaim the faith within the framework of new cultural situations. Many traditionally Catholic ways of thinking, speaking, and acting derive from the secular culture of the past, including the Hellenism of late antiquity and the classicism of medieval and early modern Europe. These cultural elements should not be unduly sacralized. Doctrinal conservatives should therefore be able to understand why some Catholics might regard the official teaching on the points we are considering as open to change.

Conversely, any progressivist who wants to be a Christian, especially a Catholic Christian, must maintain roots in the past. Christians worship the eternal Son of God, who became flesh some two thousand years ago and proclaimed a Gospel that subsequent generations gladly make their own. Christians seek to regulate their ideas and conduct by a revelation that became complete in the apostolic age and is authoritatively transmitted through the scriptures of the Old and New Testaments and through apostolic tradition. The articles of the creed and the dogmas of the church, while they admit of reformulation and reinterpretation, are abidingly true and cannot be nullified by any future developments. All Catholics should therefore be able to see why the Catholic teaching on contraception and women's ordination appears to many as irrevocable.

Conservatives and progressives who profess the Catholic faith have an additional resource for mutual understanding in their common allegiance to a church that is hierarchical and Roman. The magisterium, which is constituted by the pope and the bishops in communion with him, is divinely commissioned to certify and proclaim the teaching of Christ on controversial questions and thereby minimize the risks of schism and heresy. The magisterium, while not infallible on all points, is assisted by the Holy Spirit and esteemed by faithful Catholics as a guide for the formation of their personal views.

THE OPTIONS

In the cases of contraception and women's ordination, as in other analogous cases that might be mentioned, the hierarchical leadership had a variety of options. The following four may be considered here:

1. to let the discussion run its course in the hope that a consensus would develop;
2. to sanction a diversity of doctrines and practices within the church;
3. to adopt a new position at variance with the tradition;
4. to reaffirm the tradition in a binding way.

The first two courses of action, which would be much the same in their effects, would have led to no little confusion. The faithful would have been left without clear guidance from the church on matters of unquestionable moment for the Christian life. In the debate about contraception the five-year interval between 1963 (when John XXIII set up the Commission for the Study of Problems of Population, the Family, and Birth) and l968 (when Paul VI finally issued his encyclical) gave rise to doubts and dissension. Many theologians, priests, and laypersons, lacking magisterial direction and deeming that a doctrinal change might be imminent, simply made up their own minds.

With regard to the possibility of women priests, Paul VI did make a number of statements beginning in 1975, but none of these was considered sufficiently authoritative to bind the assent of the faithful. Meanwhile, the movement favoring women's ordination gathered momentum. The teaching of John Paul II in *Mulieris dignitatem* and other documents was widely ignored, as was that of the *Catechism of the Catholic Church*. There was a real danger, under the circumstances, that some bishop might attempt to ordain a woman and claim that the ordination was valid by divine law. This is what happened in the Protestant Episcopal Church in 1974, when four bishops illicitly ordained eleven women in Philadelphia. If such a breach of discipline had occurred in the Catholic Church, great confusion about the validity of the sacraments would have followed. To prevent this eventuality it seemed imperative to determine, on the highest authoritative level, whether or not women could be validly ordained as priests. The pope was in the position to issue such a decision and did so in 1994. Appealing to the constant and unanimous tradition and to his own authority as successor of Peter, he called upon all the Catholic faithful to give a definitive assent.

In theory, the magisterium in either case could have chosen the third option: to change the doctrine. Some Catholics regarded this as possible and desirable. But neither the advocates of change nor their theological opponents had any official mandate to speak for the church. No amount of theological discussion could relieve the magisterium of its responsibility to make a doctrinal determination.

In neither of our two cases did the decision rest on personal preference. The question was not what the Catholic people or the pope wanted but only what was permitted by divine law or divine institution. It was decided in the one case that divine law unalterably prohibited contraception and in the other case that Christ, for reasons on which we can speculate, had instituted an exclusively male priesthood. Judging that gender belonged to the very nature of the sacrament as it had been instituted, the popes taught that the church had no power to ordain women.

The spontaneous reaction of the faithful to papal pronouncements of this kind should normally be one of assent. The slogan *Roma locuta, causa finita* (Rome has spoken, the issue is settled) has long been regarded as epitomizing the Catholic attitude. Faith is, after all, submission to the word of another— that is to say, the word of God as spoken to the community through divinely commissioned and assisted representatives. Without submission to the hierarchical church, as it speaks through bishops, popes, and councils, Catholic faith would rapidly unravel. The fact that specious objections can be mounted, whether from reason or from certain biblical texts, proves nothing against the church's teaching. Every major heresy has been able to find some apparent vindication in the Bible and in philosophical reason.

EFFECTIVENESS

A further question has to do with the effectiveness of the teaching. An effective teacher, it is often said, is one who succeeds in persuading others. In the two cases we are considering, the papal magisterium has had rather limited success in winning over the assent even of Catholics, not to mention persons who do not belong to the church. Does this prove that the magisterium should have been exercised differently?

It is possible that more care should have been taken to prepare people for the doctrinal pronouncements and that the presentations might have been transmitted in a more attractive and persuasive style. Without allocating blame, one may judge that it was unfortunate that expectations for doctrinal change were allowed to rise as high as they did before the negative determinations were issued. In retrospect, it might have been better if Paul VI had spoken more promptly on birth control, without waiting several years for the report of the study commission and without deliberating two additional years after receiving that report. It might have been better, also, if the bishops of countries like our own had not allowed women's ordination conferences to proceed as though Catholic doctrine on that point were open to change.

Even so, it must be recognized that the primary task of ecclesiastical authority is to give testimony to the truth rather than to persuade. Jesus himself was not notably successful in convincing the Jews of his day, or even his chosen disciples, of his "hard sayings" on the Eucharist and on his coming passion. Paul in his Areopagus sermon did not convince many Athenians of the resurrection. To judge from his epistles, he seems to have felt that he had largely failed to communicate his doctrine of justification to the Corinthians and the Galatians.

If the church is called to be a sign of contradiction, it cannot measure its performance by the criterion of worldly success. Timothy is instructed to preach the word not only in season but also out of season (2 Tm 4:2). Even in the face of hearers who will not endure sound teaching, but accumulate teachers to suit their own liking, the evangelist is obliged to bear unwavering witness (2 Tm 4:3–5). The Catholic Church in our time is blessed by having courageous teachers who do not tailor their message to suit the preferences of their audiences. A church that trims its doctrine to the tastes and opinions of the public is a useless encumbrance, as Jesus implied when he spoke of the salt that had lost its savor (Mt 5:13).

If one assumes, as I do, the correctness of the papal teachings on issues such as contraception, abortion, assisted suicide, homosexuality, marriage and divorce, clerical celibacy, and women's ordination, it may be doubted whether there is any way of presenting the true doctrine that will win general acceptance. The whole tendency of secular public opinion is to inculcate the opposite views. A broader process of consultation might have made it even more difficult for the church to stand up against the pressure to be silent or to forsake its tradition. The rank-and-file Catholic, immersed in the social currents of the day and manipulated to some degree by the dominant opinion-makers, will inevitably experience severe tension in adhering to the Catholic tradition on these controversial issues.

POLICY IN FACE OF DISSENT

For the reasons just explained, it is not surprising that the teaching on contraception and women's ordination is not universally welcomed. On the grassroots level it is not so much a question of dissent as of ignorance. To accept church teaching one has to be exposed to credible presentations of it. Catholics who hardly know the doctrines of their church except through the fragmentary and often biased reporting of the secular media can scarcely be expected to assent in difficult cases.

Should acceptance of teachings such as those on contraception and women's ordination be required for access to the sacraments and full communion with the Catholic Church? Many theologians, seeking to answer this question, take the main issue to be that of infallibility. Since these teachings are not infallible, they say, room for dissent exists within the church. This assumption may explain some of the uproar that followed Cardinal Ratzinger's declaration in 1995 that the restriction of the ministerial priesthood to men was infallible. The very word *infallible* has become for many a red flag. It calls up images of anathemas and inquisitions.

In considering the canonical effects of these doctrines one would do better to attend to the hierarchy of truths. Are these points, even if objectively infallible, so central that their denial may be taken as a sign that Catholic faith and communion are lacking? The empirical evidence tends to show that many Catholics who accept the scriptures, the creeds, and the dogmas of the church, and who pray and worship in the community of faith, are not convinced of the two doctrines here under discussion. They do not see the doctrines as so clearly linked with God's revelation in Christ that their denial amounts to a renunciation of Catholic faith and communion.

If the popes had proclaimed these doctrines *ex cathedra*, with all the solemnities of a dogmatic definition, ecclesiastical censures might be inevitable. But in their pastoral wisdom they judged such solemn proclamations not to be opportune in these two cases. Perhaps they did not wish to force Catholics who were strongly committed to the opposed positions to choose between abandoning their honest convictions and renouncing their Catholic allegiance.

For the present, therefore, it seems that the church is prepared to tolerate doubt and nondisruptive dissent on the two doctrines we are considering. The Pontifical Council on the Family, in its 1997 *Vademecum* (Instruction) for confessors, even while declaring that the Catholic teaching on the intrinsic evil of contraception is "definitive and irreformable," advises confessors to let penitents remain in good faith in cases of subjectively invincible ignorance.[1] The same principle, I suggest, may be applied to Catholics who in good faith believe that women could be ordained to the priesthood. There is no need to demand a positive profession of belief from every Catholic as if the doctrine were an article of the creed.

This policy of lenience, however, might not extend to bishops, who hold magisterial office and administer the sacrament of orders, or to professors who teach in sensitive positions with a canonical mission from the church. To be consistent, the church cannot proclaim one position as definitively true and authorize those who speak in its name to teach the contrary.

Conclusion

Dissent is nothing new. In spite of repeated condemnations, Manichaean and Pelagian tendencies plagued the church throughout the early centuries, as did the Jansenist and Gallican movements in early modern times. The social teaching of Leo XIII encountered strident opposition. Following Vatican II the bitterest dissent has come from right-wing traditionalists. In the long run, parties that contest the official teaching of popes and councils fade into insignificance, but it may take centuries for the futility of their protest to become manifest. In some cases the magisterium profits from carefully considered criticism coming from faithful and obedient Catholics in order to nuance traditional doctrine.

If history has anything to teach us, it is that sound developments of doctrine are not fostered by defiant opposition or by the use of pressure tactics against the hierarchy. It must also be recognized that Catholic doctrine is transmitted by a tradition that develops organically under the vigilance of the ecclesiastical magisterium. Without the continuity of tradition and the fidelity of the pastors the flock of Christ could not be maintained in unity and in the truth from which it draws its life.

Note

[1] See *Origins* 26 (March 13, 1997): 617–25, at 621.

2

AUTHORITY AND ITS EXERCISE

Joseph A. Komonchak

I was asked to consider exercises of authority at the level of the episcopal conference and of this to ask three questions:

1. Who has the right to exercise authority, and on what grounds?
2. How is the decision to be made, the authority to be exercised, for it to be authentic and genuine?
3. To what extent should a decision be made at all as opposed to allowing for individual or group freedom or a pluralism of expression and action?[1]

I will address these questions primarily with regard to teaching authority and keeping in mind as examples the two famous pastoral letters of the National Conference of Catholic Bishops.[2]

THE U.S. BISHOPS' PASTORAL LETTERS

Following the example of *Gaudium et spes*, Vatican II's *Pastoral Constitution on the Church in the Modern World*, the pastoral letters make three kinds of statements. The first are "universally binding moral principles"; the second are statements from the ordinary teaching of the church; and the third are "applications of these principles" to specific issues. The principles are said to be of greater "moral authority" than the applications, which, "while not binding in conscience, are to be given serious attention and consideration by Catholics as they determine whether their moral judgments are consistent with the Gospel" (CP 9–10). The differences between these two levels are set out well in EJ 134–35:

> In focusing on some of the central economic issues and choices in American life in the light of moral principles, we are aware that the movement from principle to policy is complex and difficult and that although moral values are essential in determining public policies, they do not dictate specific solutions. They must interact with empirical data, with historical, social, and political realities, and with competing demands on limited resources. The soundness of our prudential judgments depends not only on the moral force of our principles, but also on the accuracy of our information and the validity of our assumptions.
>
> Our judgments and recommendations on specific economic issues, therefore, do not carry the same moral authority as our statements of universal moral principles and formal church teaching; the former are related to circumstances which can change or which can be interpreted differently by people of good will. We expect and welcome debate on our specific policy recommendations. Nevertheless, we want our statements on these matters to be given serious consideration by Catholics as they determine whether their own moral judgments are consistent with the Gospel and with Catholic social teaching.

This is well and modestly said. The bishops are speaking as bishops: as those who bear the religious truths and moral demands of the Gospel forward into our day and bring them to bear on two sets of very important issues. They write as pastoral leaders, not as technicians. But like Vatican II, they did not wish to remain at the level of universal and perhaps abstract principle but rather to provide more specific guidance. And, again like Vatican II, they acknowledge that "pastoral" moral teaching differs from teaching general moral principles and refrain from drawing the same clear and direct lines between the former and the Gospel that they draw between the latter and the Gospel. The general principles are "binding" in a way that the applied teaching is not.

Both documents were written at a time when Catholics—and other Americans—sharply disagreed among themselves on the two sets of issues addressed in the letters. This was clear as the bishops, preparing to write the two letters, engaged in a widespread consultation of laypeople, priests and religious, and experts in the two areas. Initial drafts of the two letters were prepared and the texts were considerably revised in the light of comments received. Contrary to some descriptions of the bishop's teaching role, the bishops made it clear that they were willing to learn before they tried to teach and that they wished the preparation of the letters to be already an ecclesial enterprise.

It was also clear that differences existed among the bishops themselves, perhaps more dramatically with regard to *The Challenge of Peace*. There were bishops who were pacifists; there were bishops who supported American nuclear policy; there was one bishop who spoke of a nuclear submarine as the "Auschwitz of Puget Sound." If any of these had published a pastoral letter in his own diocese, it would probably have been quite different from the final text, which passed with an over-whelming majority, reached after the long process of conver-sation, conciliation, and compromise. One suspects that the eagerness with which individual bishops urged it upon their own dioceses greatly differed.

The writing of *The Challenge of Peace* also involved the U.S. bishops in tensions with bishops of other countries who were also addressing the problem at the time. A curious rever-sal of roles was observed. At Vatican II it was U.S. bishops who objected to a draft of *Gaudium et spes* that would have called into question U.S. nuclear policy, while European bishops generally supported it. During the preparation of *The Challenge of Peace* it was European bishops who objected to the implications of a draft of the U.S. bishops' document for European security interests. Rome, too, became concerned and sponsored a meeting at which representatives of the interested episcopates met to discuss their differences. These conversations also led to changes in the text.

Not everyone was happy with the final results, of course, and in particular not with the applications of principle that required the bishops to judge and choose among various accumulations of data; various assessments of situations; various political, strategic, or economic theories; and various policy proposals. (The grounds of these choices were not set out in the letters.) I do not know whether any study has been done of the impact of the letters on Catholic views or on the general political culture. My impression is that a good number of those who favored assessments, theories, or proposals not in the end chosen to guide the bishops' applications and recommendations were not greatly moved by the bishops' choices in these areas. In fact, "counter pastoral letters" were published in reply to the pastoral letters. We are here dealing with the question of the *reception* of the letters, the question, that is, of their *effective* authority, which is distinct from the question of their *de iure* authority.

With regard to *The Challenge of Peace*, it would appear that a difference on the level of principle was left unresolved, or rather, it was resolved by being reduced to a difference in "method" or "perception": I mean the difference between Christian pacifism and Christian just war theory (see *CP* 73–74, 120–21). Proponents of pacifism were left dissatisfied with the letter's endorsement of the right of nations to use force in self-defense, while some advocates of the latter regretted the letter's statement that the two "perspectives" were "complementary."

Both letters attracted a good deal of attention in the secular press, where, however, the attention often fell, it seems, not upon the statements of Christian moral principles but upon the specific applications and recommendations. The Reagan administration certainly took an interest in *The Challenge of Peace* when it was being written and tried to exert some influence. I do not know whether the final text of either letter had any effect upon the ideas or actions of politicians or economists and businessmen.

SOME REFLECTIONS AND QUESTIONS

1. Episcopal conferences are located between the individual bishop, "a visible principle and basis of unity in an individual church," and the pope, "a visible principle and basis of unity for the whole church" (see *LG* 23). *Lumen gentium* sets out clearly the teaching authority of bishops and pope: "Bishops teaching in communion with the Roman Pontiff should be respected by all as witnesses to divine and catholic truth; and what they teach in the name of Christ on matters of faith and morals the faithful should accept and adhere to it with a religious assent of their minds" (*LG* 25). The same assent is singularly due to the ordinary teachings of the pope. Although individual bishops cannot speak with infallible authority, when they all, whether gathered in ecumenical council or scattered throughout the world, agree upon a teaching that must be definitively held by all, they infallibly teach the doctrine of Christ. This infallibility also attends certain exercises of the authority of the Roman pontiff.

The council said nothing explicit about a teaching role for episcopal conferences; and at the very time the U.S. bishops were preparing these two pastoral letters, there was a vigorous debate among canonists and theologians as to whether episcopal conferences have a distinct teaching authority or not.[3] Both the council in *Christus dominus* 38 and the new *Code of Canon*

Law make it clear that, under certain conditions, an episcopal conference has legislative authority; that is, it can pass laws which are binding upon the individual bishop-members of the conference and also upon the body of the faithful under their care. It was not clear that the conference could also teach with an authority superior to that of the bishops taken singly. Opinions were split on the issue. A Roman "Working Paper" on episcopal conferences sent out to bishops in 1988 was rather negative on the question; and while a committee was formed to revise the "Working Paper," no further document on the question has come from Rome since.[4]

My own view is that it would be odd to assign the powerful teaching authority described in *Lumen gentium* 25 to the individual bishop and to deny it to a regional or national group of bishops.[5] Historically, local and regional councils (ancient analogues of the episcopal conferences) have been acknowledged to have teaching roles; and I should think, on good ecclesiological and sociological grounds, that the agreement of "two or three," never mind two or three hundred, might be considered antecedently to carry greater weight than that of a single bishop.

The problem seems to reside in the uncertain juridical character of episcopal conferences, poised between what some canonists and theologians regard as the only two offices that exist in the church by divine right: the episcopal and the papal. At the council there was a debate as to whether intermediary bodies, such as the ancient patriarchate or the modern episcopal conference, share that dignity. *Lumen gentium* 23 used vaguer language of the patriarchates when it said that they had developed "by divine Providence" and when it said, at the end of the same paragraph, that "similarly, episcopal conferences today can make a manifold and fruitful contribution so that the collegial awareness (*collegialis affectus*) can be concretely applied."[6] Disagreements at the council over whether episcopal conferences represent an exercise of collegiality led to the decision to leave the question open, so that *Christus dominus* 38 was content to say more vaguely that in them "bishops of a given nation or territory jointly (*conjunctim*) exercise their pastoral office."

After the council the view emerged that episcopal conferences represent an instance of *affective* collegiality, which is to be distinguished from *effective* collegiality, the latter being the only "true" and "strict" expression of collegiality and requiring the action of the universal body of bishops. I believe that this distinction, which is in danger of becoming canonical, is foreign to both the intentions and the words of Vatican II.[7] The view, expressed at the council by many prominent bishops, canonists, and theologians and neither endorsed nor rejected in the final texts—namely, that episcopal conferences represent an expression of genuine collegiality—may still be held.

2. It is customary in Catholic circles to translate the question of teaching authority into the question of the "binding force" of episcopal or papal teachings. Perhaps we should not overlook the oddness of this language, which is well illustrated in the phrase "*obeying* a church *teaching*." In all other cases, it seems, we ordinarily refer not to *obeying* a teaching but to *agreeing with* or *assenting to* a teaching; one gives obedience to laws or commands. The act expected in response to a teaching is a judgment, an assent of the mind, and it remains that even when it is not compelled by evidence but results from a moral judgment of the reasonableness and duty of believing on the basis of authority and from the decision to believe. The common Catholic phrase oversimplifies this process and assigns the verb *obeying* to the object to which we are expected to *assent*.

This slippage is facilitated by the not uncommon habit of assimilating teaching in the church to legislating, as in one classical canonical view that teaching is a subspecies of jurisdiction; and this becomes still more problematic when law itself is interpreted voluntaristically, as if its binding force depended less on the reasonableness of an enactment than on the will of the legislator. This view was summed up in the words of a Reformation-era theologian, Thomas Stapleton, frequently quoted and criticized by Yves Congar: "When it comes to matters of faith, Catholics should ask, not what is being said, but who is speaking."

It is not uncommon to draw a sharp contrast between the nature and exercise of teaching authority in the church by pope and bishops and other instances and exercises of teaching authority, as, for example, when the church's *magisterium authenticum* (authoritative or official magisterium) is contrasted with the *magisterium scientificum* (scientific or scholarly magisterium) everywhere else, or when the former is said to be authoritative in virtue of an office and the latter in virtue of the reasons the scholar offers. It is thus said that the teaching of pope or bishop has an authority that is independent of the reasons offered for the teaching. This rule has often been applied for the interpretation of the dogmas of ecumenical councils, and it was invoked by Pius XII on behalf of the ordinary magisterium of the pope.[8] It is enough that the enactment come from the empowered office.

A good deal of the discussion of the teaching authority of episcopal conferences has occurred within this context of formal authority and of its consequence for the faithful: the obligation to assent.

3. I would like to suggest that a purely formal approach to authority is insufficient for the kind of discussion we are expected to initiate here. In addition to a discussion of the formal or de iure grounds of authority, we need to discuss also the conditions of effective or de facto authority, which I believe reduce considerably the often-claimed uniqueness of teaching authority in the church.

I will begin with two quotations, the first from the Rev. Mark S. Sisk in 1997.

"I think authority today tends to be conferred by those that are in the community, rather than something that is automatically assumed by the office," he said. "In fact, the bishop has often much less real power than is often believed."

"In that case, the ability to lead comes from being considered trustworthy, competent and respectful of one's flock," he said.[9]

My second quotation comes from a letter that John Henry Newman wrote to the father of a young man whom Newman had just received into the church:

Nor do I feel, as I should perhaps if I were you, that he is putting himself under a sort of intellectual tyranny by doing an act which he is not allowed to reverse. The ecclesiastical prohibition to doubt and inquire is not so much a practical rule as a scientific principle, which is laid down to make the theological system consistent with itself. A Catholic is kept from skepticism, not by any external prohibition, but by admiration, trust, and love. While he admires, trusts, and loves our Lord and His church, those feelings prohibit him from doubt; they guard and protect his faith; the real prohibition is from within. But suppose those feelings go; suppose he ceases to have admiration, trust, and love, of Our Lord and His church; in that case, the external prohibition probably will not suffice to keep him from doubting, if he be of an argumentative turn.

Thus it avails in neither case; while he loves and trusts, it is not needed; when he does not love and trust, it is impotent.

I expect that, as Eddy experiences more and more what the Catholic Religion is, its power, strength, comfort, peace, and depth, the greater devotion will he have towards it, as the gift of God, and the greater repugnance to put it on its trial, as if he had never heard of it. To bid him authoritatively not to doubt, will be as irrelevant, as to tell him not to maim himself or put his eyes out.[10]

Bishop-elect Sisk is talking about effective authority and maintains that it is conferred by the community on one considered to be "trustworthy, competent, and respectful of one's flock." The conferral of such authority, "the ability to lead," is not guaranteed by the office assumed but requires (presumably demonstrated) trustworthiness, competence, and respectfulness.

These views are not utterly foreign to the Catholic view of ministry in the church. We have a lengthy and at least once exigent process for training people for the priesthood, and the *Code of Canon Law* both sets out the qualities required in a pastor (c. 521 §2) and includes among the reasons for which he can be removed "incompetence" and "the loss of a good reputation among upright and good parishioners or aversion to the pastor which are foreseen as not ceasing in a short time" (c. 1741 §2–3).[11] Similarly, the code lists the qualities required in a bishop, which include "the talents which make him fit to fulfill the office," "a good reputation," and either a degree or expertise in scripture, theology, or canon law (c. 378, §1–2); it does not, however, give a list of reasons for the removal of a bishop. The code offers no such list, either of qualifications or of reasons for removal, in the case of the pope, but a millennium of discussion can be cited of what the church should do in the case of a heretical pope.[12] These are all different ways of spelling out that the exercise of authority ("the ability to lead") requires trustworthiness, competence, and respectfulness, and they can ground a judgment in principle that authority is not simply assured in virtue of an office but is also conferred by the community.

Newman emphasizes the ecclesial conditions within which authority exists and which are required for it to be acknowledged and respected: "admiration, trust, and love" for Christ and the church. When these are present, external prohibition or authoritative command is unnecessary; when they are absent, it is ineffective. If, in fact, exercises of teaching authority in the church, whether by pope, bishop, or episcopal conference, are today ineffective, Newman's remarks might usefully turn our attention beyond questions of formal authority to consider how to restore the admiration, trust, and love that it presupposes for its effective exercise.

I am struck by the presence in both quotations of the word *trust*. Elsewhere I have argued that real or effective authority is a social relationship in which one person trusts another person to provide intelligent, reasonable, and responsible guidance in some area of common interest.[13] In book reviews we may read that an author is an "authority" on a subject, that a book is an "authoritative" treatment of a subject, that a translation is "authoritative"; and in each case the reviewer is saying that the author, book, or translation may be trusted. (Notice that we may also find ourselves trusting the reviewer, which is why we are grateful when his or her credentials [trustworthiness] are given in a note.) Teachers in our schools, colleges, or universities are said to be "authorities" in their fields, which means that they are trustworthy. Let us reflect for a moment on this latter case.

Teachers enjoy effective authority because their students believe or trust that they know what they are talking about. The grounds of this belief may vary: the students may have heard about certain teachers or read their books. More likely they attend their classes because they happen to be teaching at the school the students are attending, and their belief in their teachers' authority derives from an assumption that the school would not have hired or retained incompetents. Behind the school's decision to hire its faculty, of course, lie their previous record: graduation, advanced degree, letters of recommendation, and so on. Behind its decision to retain certain teachers lie demonstrated abilities and performance. In most cases the antecedent trust with which the student listens to his or her teachers and expects to learn from them rests upon trust in the institution and the procedures that have placed these persons in a teaching position.

I'll share an example from my own experience. When I have begun a class on the Second Vatican Council with the statement: "On January 25, 1959, less than 100 days after his election, Pope John XXIII startled the Catholic world by announcing that he intended to convoke an ecumenical council," I have (so far, at least!) never been challenged: "What is the evidence for this? Prove it!" And I know of no student who rushed to the library to verify the several elements in my statement. Even if a student were so inclined, of course, the effort to validate my statement would require a whole set of other acts of faith: in contemporary reports, works of history, the accuracy of official *acta*, and so forth. But my statement in fact is simply believed, and reasonably and responsibly believed, on the basis of my authority. Students who take the class and think they have learned something leave it *believing*, not *knowing* by their own independent research, well over 90 percent of what they think they learned and think they now "know."

The antecedent trust, of course, can be disappointed, as when it becomes clear that a teacher does not know what he or she is talking about. The school, when it discovers this, may admit its mistake and for the sake of future trust in itself dismiss the teacher—unless, of course, the teacher has tenure! Schools that have enough of such teachers will eventually cease to attract students. Students, when they discover that the teacher does not deserve it, will suspend their antecedent trust and eventually the teacher will have no students.

You will notice that teachers' authority rests first upon the office they occupy. It is because the school is trusted that the teachers are trusted. Because the teachers are trusted, it is not necessary for them to parade all the reasons they have for their every statement. It will be necessary for teachers, however, if questioned or challenged, to be able to supply the reasons; regular inability to supply them will lead to the conclusion that such a teacher should not be trusted, is not an "authority."

I think there are more similarities between this and the situation of official teachers in the church than are commonly acknowledged. The offices in question are believed by the church to be willed by Christ and promised the assistance of his Spirit, different grounds, that is, from those that underlie other offices elsewhere. But the code's requirements for the training of priests and for election to episcopal office make it very clear that the divine establishment and guidance of those offices do not suffice; it is also necessary that they be occupied by men who are themselves worthy of the trust that Catholics first place in the offices themselves and only derivatively in those who occupy them. Should these men be shown to be grossly unworthy of that trust, they can be replaced. If such persons are not replaced, eventually the offices themselves are likely to cease to be trusted.

There are also similarities with respect to the relationship between the formal office of pope or bishop and the performance of those who exercise those roles and the relationship between the formal office of other teachers and their performance. Timothy was urged to appoint as a bishop only a man who was "not quarrelsome but kindly to everyone, an apt teacher, patient, correcting opponents with gentleness" (2 Tm 2:24; see 1 Tm 3:2ff.), and this because of the other injunction: "What you have heard from me through many witnesses entrust to faithful people who will be able to teach others as well" (2 Tm 2:2). The divinely established and guided office requires "apt teachers," capable of handing on what they have received. Obviously, aptness as a teacher requires the apostolic faith—that the teacher know what to teach; and this is respected in the requirement that a man, before he is ordained, make a profession of faith and in the age-old discussion of what to do in the case of a heretical pope. But it is also clear that the teacher should also know how to teach, that is, not in a quarrelsome way, but patiently and gently (compare 1 Pt 3:15: "Always be ready to make your defense to anyone who demands from you an accounting for the hope that is in you; yet do it with gentleness and reverence"). Continued trust in the office itself requires that it regularly be occupied by people who know both what to teach and how to teach it. Even in the church, a teaching office that is regularly filled by people who are not "apt teachers" will eventually cease to be trusted.

This is the reason why mere appeals to formal authority of office cannot suffice. Everything should work fine if in offices that ought to be trusted there are people who can be trusted and the faithful are themselves properly trusting. But other possibilities are possible and have in fact been realized. Trustworthy people may occupy trustworthy offices, and then it is wrong not to trust them. Untrustworthy people may occupy trustworthy offices, and it may be wrong to trust them. Putting it more simply, some people who do not deserve trust are trusted, and some people who deserve trust are not trusted. This is the reason why the church's strength rests finally upon the work of God's Spirit both in officeholders and in those subject to them. There is no substitute, not even the formal structures of divinely established and guided offices, for God's grace and the conversion it effects.

Newman had some very pertinent comments:

Consider the Bible tells us to be meek, humble, single-hearted and teachable. Now, it is plain that humility and teachableness are qualities of mind necessary for arriving at the truth in any subject, and in religious matters as well as others. By obeying Scripture, then in practicing humility and teachableness, it is evident that we are at least *in the way* to arrive at the knowledge of God. On the other hand, impatient, proud, self-confident, obstinate men are generally wrong in the opinions they form of persons and things. Prejudice and self-conceit blind the eyes and mislead the judgment, whatever be the subject inquired into. . . . The same thing happens also in religious inquiries. When I see a person hasty and violent, harsh and high-minded, careless of what others feel, and disdainful of what they think—when I see such a one proceeding to inquire into religious subjects, I am sure beforehand that he cannot go right—he will not be led into all the truth—it is contrary to the nature of things and the experience of the world, that he should find what he is seeking. I should say the same were he seeking to find out what to believe or to do in any other matter not religious, but especially in any such important and solemn inquiry; for the *fear* of the Lord (humbleness, teachableness, reverence towards Him) is the very *beginning* of wisdom, as Solomon tells us; it leads us to think over things modestly and humbly, to examine patiently, to bear doubt and uncertainty, to wait perseveringly for an increase of light, to be slow to speak, and to be deliberate in deciding.[14]

It would not be unusual, or inappropriate, to apply these words to the faithful as a description of the virtues required in religious inquiry and of the attitudes that they ought to have also toward those in authority. It is less common to draw attention to the prior sense of admiration, trust, and love of the church, the appreciation of its "power, strength, comfort, peace, and depth," that, on the one hand, make it more probable that the faithful will have the proper virtues and attitudes toward authority and, on the other hand, effectively define the place of formal or external authority, rendering it in the one case unnecessary and superfluous and in the other insufficient and impotent. If such admiration, trust, and love are not as widely present as one might desire, then the first thing to be attempted must be to restore them, and one of the conditions for this is that the holders of offices of authority themselves display the kinds of virtues Newman described.[15] All of which is to say that there are limits to what authority can accomplish by itself and that so far from existing in order to substitute, either in officeholders or in others, for grace, conversion, or authenticity, it requires these in both groups.[16]

4. There remains a final condition: that authority not make claims outside the areas in which it is trustworthy. Students do not take my classes in order to learn about physics. One of the questions raised with regard to the U.S. bishops' pastoral letters was their competence in the two areas. The issue was put rather rudely to me when I began a class on the church and social issues by mentioning that the bishops were preparing a document on the U.S. economy. A student immediately exclaimed, "What do bishops know about economics?" On the one hand, he may have been of the view that economics is a science to which religious or even moral matters are extraneous

or of the view that religion has nothing to say about economics. On the other hand, he may have been raising the question about how much bishops actually do know about economics.

To their credit the U.S. bishops acknowledged that their moral authority was greater in the sections on biblical and church teaching with regard to the principles affecting war and peace and economics than in the sections on policy decisions. Put in terms of my analysis here, this simply means that what they say in the first sections is on antecedent grounds more trustworthy than what they say in the second sections.

Notes

[1] I note the absence of any question about the rights and duties of those under authority or about the general cultural and ecclesial attitude toward authority and authorities, particularly assumptions that power and authority are the same thing and that both should be counterposed to freedom.

[2] *The Challenge of Peace: God's Promise and Our Response* (May 3, 1983) and *Economic Justice for All: Pastoral Letter on Catholic Social Teaching and the U.S. Economy* (November 18, 1986). I will cite these texts by paragraph number.

[3] See Avery Dulles, "Doctrinal Authority of Episcopal Conferences," and Ladislas Orsy, "Reflections on the Teaching Authority of the Episcopal Conferences," in *Episcopal Conferences: Historical, Canonical, and Theological Studies*, ed. T. J. Reese (Washington, D.C.: Georgetown University Press, 1989), 207-52; Julio Manzanares, "The Teaching Authority of Episcopal Conferences," and Ricardo Blazquez, "The Weight of the Concordant Witness of Bishops," in *The Nature and Future of Episcopal Conferences*, ed. H. Legrand et al. (Washington, D.C.: Catholic University of America Press, 1988), 234-69.

[4] Ed. Note: An apostolic letter, *Apostolos suos*, was issued by the Congregation for the Doctrine of the Faith with the approval of John Paul II on May 21, 1998, addressing this question.

[5] I may perhaps note here that these claims for individual bishops receive hardly any attention in the literature on the magisterium since the council. They are not mentioned, for example, in the "Instruction

on the Ecclesial Vocation of the Theologian," issued by the Congregation for the Doctrine of the Faith in 1990.

[6] *Lumen gentium* 23 begins with the words "collegialis unio" (collegial union or unity) and ends with the words "affectus collegialis." I believe that the terms have the same objective reference and that the latter should not be interpreted as if it referred to affections or emotions. I owe the insight to remarks of the Italian historian Vittorio Peri on the meaning of *affectus* in classical Latin. He would translate *affectus collegialis* as "the awareness that they constitute a college."

[7] For the argument, see Joseph A. Komonchak, "The Roman Working Paper on Episcopal Conferences," in Reese, *Episcopal Conferences,* 188-95.

[8] When Etienne Gilson, upset that a book by another great medieval scholar, M-D. Chenu, had been placed on the Index, inquired of the-then-Msgr. Giovanni Battisti Montini about what doctrinal errors had been found in it, Montini replied: "Le propre de l'autorite, c'est de ne pas se justifier" (The distinguishing mark of authority is that it doesn't justify itself). See Laurence K. Shook, *Etienne Gilson* (Toronto: Pontifical Institute of Medieval Studies, 1984), 248.

[9] Remarks of the Rev. Mark S. Sisk, recently elected bishop coadjutor of the New York Diocese of the Episcopal Church, as quoted in *The New York Times,* November 8, 1997, A13.

[10] *The Letters and Diaries of John Henry Newman,* vol. 20 (London: Nelson, 1970), 430-31; see also 425: "Denunciation neither effects subjection in thought nor in conduct. . . . You cannot make men believe by force and repression. Were the Holy See as powerful in temporals, as it was three centuries back, then you would have a secret infidelity instead of an *avowed* one—(which seems the worse evil) unless you train the reason to defend the truth. Galileo subscribed what was asked of him, but is said to have murmured, 'E pur muove' [And yet it moves]."

[11] The 1917 *Code,* c. 2147 §2, had spoken of the "hatred of the people [*odium populi*], even if unjust and not universal, so long as it is such as to impede the pastor's useful ministry and is not foreseen as ceasing in a short time."

[12] The discussion focused on the Decretist text (Diet. 40, c. 6): "*Cunctos ipse iudicaturus a nemine est iudi-candus, nisi deprehendatur a fide devius*" (The Roman Pontiff, who is to judge all, is not to be

judged by anyone else, unless he should be discovered to have departed from the faith).

[13] Joseph Komonchak, "Authority and Magisterium," in *Vatican Authority and American Catholic Dissent*, ed. William W. May (New York: Crossroad, 1987), 103-14.

[14] John Henry Newman, "Inward Witness to the Truth of the Gospel," in *Parochial and Plain Sermons*, vol. 7 (London: Longmans, Green and Co., 1891), 113–14.

[15] One is reminded of the remark of Bernard Lonergan, discussing the question of pluralism and unity: "But the real menace to unity of faith . . . lies in the absence of intellectual or moral or religious conversion," which becomes particularly perilous "when the absence of conversion occurs in those that govern the church or teach in its name" (*Method in Theology* [New York: Herder and Herder, 1972], 330). The literature on this subject is not vast.

[16] Speaking of infallible teachings, Vatican II said that "the assent of the Church to such definitions can never be lacking because of the Holy Spirit, by whose assistance the definitions are immune from error and by whose action the whole flock of Christ adheres to them and also makes progress in faith" *(LG 25)*. A proposed amendment that would have made the church's assent follow from the formal authority of the pope or ecumenical council was rejected by the Doctrinal Commission on the grounds that "the principle of the church's unity is the assistance of the Holy Spirit" (*Acta Synodalia*, III.VIII [Typis Polyglottis Vaticanis 1976], 92).

3

CHURCH AUTHORITY IN AMERICAN CULTURE

Cases and Observations

James A. Coriden

INTRODUCTION

This reflection centers on discipline rather than doctrine. It is concerned with the exercise of the power of governance (*potestas regiminis*) and not teaching authority. Canonists distinguish the power of governance into the three traditional categories of legislative, executive, and judicial[1]; however, the three are not separated but united in the office of a diocesan bishop. Still, bishops rarely make laws, and they usually delegate their judicial authority to the judges in their tribunals. Hence the focus here is on the executive or administrative authority exercised by bishops and pastors in the ordinary course of their ministry.

This authority must be envisioned within an ecclesial context. It is necessary to distinguish its exercise within the *church* community from that within other institutions of our culture. A bishop's authority differs from that of a city mayor, a corporation executive, or an army officer. A pastor's exercise of authority is unlike that of a surgeon in an operating room, or of a football coach, or of an academic dean. The extent and style of administrative leadership depends on its context, and its setting within the church conditions it radically.

The Roman Catholic Church in the United States has its own ethos of authority. It differs somewhat from other Christian churches, and even from Catholic churches elsewhere in the world. While it is not uniform in its expectations or manners from coast to coast, still it is notably unlike that in the Methodist or Baptist or Lutheran churches, and even unlike that found in the Catholic churches in other cultures, as in parts of Africa and Asia. Diverse factors influence this ethos, for example, a Catholic sense of what communion implies, high esteem for the episcopal office, American individualism.

One more introductory note. Christians cannot even begin to discuss authority in the church without reflecting on its essential counterpart, freedom. Christian freedom is not simply a correlative term; it is a very profound concept, an absolutely bedrock biblical category. Jesus said that "the truth will make you free" (Jn 8:31), Paul spoke of "the freedom of the glory of the children of God" (Rom 8:21), and James wrote about "the perfect law, the law of liberty" (Jas 1:25). These are not mere rhetorical flourishes; they point to a basic Christian truth. This freedom in Christ means a saving deliverance from sin and death but also freedom from what the Mosaic law had become, and from similarly enslaving human regulations. Freedom is central to the law of grace, the new law of the Spirit. It was revived by the Second Vatican Council's teachings on religious freedom and on the primacy of conscience.[2]

CASES

The following three cases involve: (1) general absolution, (2) reconciliation of the divorced and remarried, and (3) conflict resolution through mediation.

In the planning for this conference it was suggested that each case be subjected to this interpretive framework: In the exercise of authority in question, (1) who had the right to make the decision? (2) how should that authority have been exercised in order to be authentic and effective? and (3) should the decision have been made at all, as over against allowing freedom of expression or action? Reflect on these issues as you consider these three cases.

Pastoral Accommodation

General absolution (that imparted to several penitents at once without previous individual confession) has roots in the "canonical penance" practiced in the early church. Sinners were received into a publicly identified "order of penitents," performed penances for a set period of time, and then reconciled as a group.[3] General absolution was restored to use during the Second World War by priests ministering in emergency situations.[4] When the rite of penance was reformed after the Second Vatican Council, general absolution was provided as one form of the sacrament.[5] However, the ritual and the 1983 code tightly circumscribe the actual use of this third form of sacramental reconciliation to (1) the imminent danger of death of a group of people, or (2) a serious necessity in which the supply of confessors and the number of penitents is such that the penitents will be deprived of sacramental grace for a long time through no fault of their own. It is for the diocesan bishop to determine whether the second set of conditions exists or not (c. 961).

Many pastors in the Archdiocese of Chicago, as elsewhere,[6] have used the third form of the sacrament of penance, general absolution, very effectively in their parishes. On February 22, 1994, Archbishop Joseph Bernardin sent a four-page letter to all the priests of the Archdiocese of Chicago, which said in part:

> In the judgment of the bishops of the Chicago Province, the conditions that would warrant general permission for this form (Form III) do not exist in the dioceses of Illinois. Authorization for imparting general absolution, therefore, is not given in the archdiocese.[7]

Sixty pastors met at Holy Name Cathedral on March 11 to discuss the archbishop's letter. They sent a report of their meeting to the archbishop, which said, among other things:

> There was respect for the Cardinal and sadness at the disarray in the church. But first and foremost, there was a profound concern that the central gospel value of God's merciful forgiveness in our lives and the integrity of our parishioners' experience of that mercy be enhanced.[8]

The report went on to detail their pastoral and theological concerns. Three of the pastors met with the archbishop to discuss the report with him personally. Another group of them planned a "pastors' forum" on the sacrament of reconciliation for September 12 and sent out a survey to all pastors about the experience of the sacrament in their parishes.

One hundred fifteen pastors responded to the survey, and a summary, which showed great diversity of practice and no unanimity among the pastors, was presented to the forum. Archbishop Bernardin was invited to the forum, and he offered his own remarks, among which:

> I feel caught in the middle between the magisterium to which I belong and am bound to support, and the pastors and their people to whom I am obliged to listen and to be a good shepherd. I see validity to both sides of the issue.[9]

The assembled pastors spoke to the issue. Some said:

> By being loyal to authorities, are we being disloyal to our people and to the gospel values involved here? From the earliest centuries, we have had unity in belief coupled with diversity in discipline.[10]

The pastors voted to have another forum on the topic, because they felt that they had learned a great deal. They appreciated the archbishop's "willingness to listen to their concerns, to express his agreement and disagreement, and to embrace a collaborative rather than authoritarian relationship. They viewed all of this as a sign of hope for the future."[11]

Archbishop Bernardin, in his final remarks at the forum, said that "he saw candid discussion of this kind as a positive sign. It would be regrettable if the bishop and his priests were completely estranged or intimidated by each other or unable to listen to and learn from each other's experience and perspective. How ironic it would be if the sacrament of reconciliation were to drive a wedge between them."[12]

Moral Discernment and Subsidiarity

In 1968 Raymond Carey of the Chicago matrimonial tribunal presented a paper at the Midwest Canon Law Workshop about a process called "the good-faith solution" to marriage cases.[13] He said that when there was some doubt about the validity of a prior marriage, and the doubt could not be resolved, the tribunal would issue a document instructing the parties' pastor to "leave them in good faith," thus permitting the parties to a stable second marriage to be admitted to the sacraments, provided that no scandal would be given thereby. It was a practice that had been in place for over twenty years with the approval of three successive archbishops.

The "good-faith decree" was not a judicial decision; it declared neither the nullity of the former marriage nor the validity of the present one. Rather, it provided the parish priest with a consultative process and afforded the couple the assurance of an official-looking document. The procedure was administrative, and the decision was "canonico-moral." However, by the late 1960s, marriage tribunals began to question the issuance of the documents and asked whether the parish priest could not assist the couple directly by helping them make what is essentially a moral decision about receiving the sacraments, consulting the tribunal by phone when advice was needed.

In 1971 a committee of the Catholic Theological Society of America studied the matter and recommended that the church's pastoral practice respect a couple's conscience. Reception of the Eucharist could be permitted to those in second marriages who present themselves "after appropriate consultation, reflection and prayer," provided that their present marriages showed evidence of fidelity and stability and that they seemed to be living good Catholic lives.[14]

In June of 1972 Bishop Robert Tracy of Baton Rouge, Louisiana, motivated by a desire to have a more uniform pastoral practice in that diocese, published a pastoral letter on "good-conscience cases" that envisioned the granting of administrative "decrees of good-conscience" to those who believed in their consciences that their first marriage was not a true marriage but that their present one is, and who feel a serious moral obligation to maintain their second union.[15] He referred to the process as "an internal forum solution" (when such a solution is reached within the sacrament of reconciliation) but it really wasn't, because it involved a written administrative process with records retained at the chancery.

The reaction to Bishop Tracy's initiative was swift and firm. Archbishop Krol, president of the NCCB, stated on August 17 that the issue of the reception of the sacraments by divorced and remarried Catholics was under study by the Holy See and by the NCCB Committee on Pastoral Research and Practices. He referred to a letter from the Holy See that made clear that "dioceses are not to introduce procedures that are contrary to current discipline" while the studies are under way.[16]

On April 11, 1973, Cardinal Seper, the prefect of the Congregation for the Doctrine of the Faith, wrote to the president of the NCCB about certain "new opinions" regarding the indissolubility of matrimony. The Congregation urged fidelity to the church's teaching and practice regarding the indissolubility of marriage. The letter concluded:

> In regard to admission to the Sacraments, the Ordinaries are asked on the one hand to stress observance of current disci-

pline and, on the other hand, to take care that the pastors of souls exercise special care to seek out those who are living in an irregular union by applying to the solution of such cases, in addition to other right means, the church's approved practice in the internal forum.[17]

The NCCB could not agree on the interpretation of the deliberately ambiguous final phrase of the letter and wrote back to request an explanation. The Congregation's response, dated March 21, 1975, came to Archbishop Bernardin as president of the NCCB. It stated that the phrase "probata praxis ecclesiae" (the church's approved practice) in reference to Catholics living in irregular marital unions "must be understood in the context of traditional moral theology. These couples may be allowed to receive the sacraments on two conditions, that they try to live according to the demands of Christian moral principles and that they receive the sacraments in churches in which they are not known so that they will not create any scandal."[18]

The U.S. bishops, through the NCCB Committee on Pastoral Research and Practices (chaired by Bishop James Hickey), attempted throughout the remainder of the 1970s to develop a national policy to ensure some uniformity of practice. They were thwarted in these efforts by interventions of "higher authority" in 1976 and 1979, which prevented the NCCB from continuing its discussion and taking action.[19]

Conflict Resolution

Father John Adams,[20] aged fifty-nine, an experienced pastor, had been the pastor of Sacred Heart Parish for ten years. He tended to be overbearing and was known to have a temper. Over the years he had hired employees and pastoral staff members, some of whom were not the strongest individuals. He treated them reasonably well in most respects, but sometimes he berated them in public. He said that he "just liked to blow off steam."

Adams requested and was granted a sabbatical leave in the first part of 1996 to study at the North American College in Rome. While he was absent the parish employees bonded more closely and shared their dissatisfaction with their pastor. Five of them together wrote to Stanley Mahonski, the bishop of Sterling, complaining about Adams's treatment of them, saying that "we can't deal with him any longer," and asking that he be replaced. The bishop, preoccupied with other matters, wrote back and said that he'd deal with the situation when Adams returned.

The five parish staff members were both irritated by the bishop's "brush-off" and alarmed at the prospect of the pastor's return. They sought out an aggressive lawyer who described Adams's actions as "serious verbal abuse in the workplace." On March 15, with the pastor due home for Easter, the staff and their lawyer demanded that the bishop remove the pastor or they would sue the diocese. They accused Adams of the intentional infliction of mental distress, and the diocese of negligent supervision. They did not ask for money damages or for any punishment of their pastor, only that he be removed from the parish.

At this point the complaint was referred to the diocesan office of due process, headed by Janet Austin. She asked the bishop to give Adams a month's extension of his sabbatical leave, which he did. She consulted with the office of priest personnel and the diocesan attorney. She met with the parish staff members and their attorney, listened to their grievances, and apologized to them in the name of the diocese for Adams's behavior; his reputation for public vituperation was well known. Austin persuaded them to enter into the diocese's internal process for dispute resolution. She told them that the court would probably insist that they exhaust that avenue of recourse before accepting their complaint anyway, because the process had been in place for years, was used regularly, and had a success rate of 80 percent of its cases. Due process was a demonstrable part of the diocesan structure, the way it does business.

Austin insisted that Father Adams be a full participant in the proceedings and provided him with able canonical counsel at diocesan expense. Austin then obtained (at substantial cost to the diocese) the services of an experienced mediator, a former judge. All parties came to the table. They "hashed it out," and the process of mediation went forward to a resolution, which, because of two months of intense preparations, was accomplished in a single day.

With the help of his canonical counsel the pastor was able to see the consequences of his actions, and he agreed to resign. Satisfied at the outcome, he is now the administrator of another parish and engaged in counseling for his problem with anger. The parish staff members were also satisfied, and, after being assisted by a facilitator, are working with a new pastor.

ON AUTHORITY IN THE CHURCH

Christian reflection on issues like freedom and authority should focus first on the common tradition, especially the biblical. There is nothing wrong with using other frameworks of analysis, like the classical sociological approach of Max Weber,[21] but the churches are obliged not to lose sight of their biblical heritage and apostolic origins. The vicissitudes of history, centuries of different church-state relations in particular, have shaped and sometimes warped the church's concepts and practices of authority. An authentic vision must include the biblical data.

The nature and manifestations of authority in the New Testament sources must be envisioned within God's salvific purpose. Authority is always seen and exercised for or unto salvation. The overarching plan of God, the saving of humankind through the life, actions, and preaching of Jesus Christ, is the scene and setting for authority. Some of its specific elements follow.

a. All power and authority in the church is derived from Christ the Lord.[22] It is made active and operative in the life of the church by the Holy Spirit.[23]

b. Jesus, during his life on earth, described the scope of his authority in various ways: authority over all people so that he could give them eternal life (Jn 17:1–2), the power to become children of God (Jn 1:12), the power to exercise judgment (Jn 5:27), the power to forgive sins (Mk 2:10–11), the power to teach with authority (Mk 1:22), power and authority (to the Twelve and the seventy-two) to cast out demons and to cure diseases (Lk 9:1; 10:1).

c. Faith was the necessary context within which Jesus exercised power, especially his miracles or "mighty deeds" (Mt 13:28; Mk 9:14ff.).

d. The community of believers drew its strength from the Lord and his mighty power (Eph 6:10) and shared in the powerful gifts of the Spirit (1 Cor 12:10, 28).

e. Jesus' teaching on authority as service is one of the strongest and clearest in the New Testament. The parallel passages in all four gospels point to an authentic saying of Jesus repeated by the evangelists for their own communities.[24] Authority as service is rooted in the identity and mission of Christ. It defines the very nature of authority in the church, not simply the style of its exercise.

The Second Vatican Council went a long way toward restoring the biblical vision of authority as service. Its most solemn discussion of authority takes place in the context of its teaching on the church. Both the placement and the content of the reflections on authority remind us that the communities of the faithful stand in first place, then the ministers in service to them:

For the nourishment and continual growth of the people of God, Christ the lord instituted a variety of ministries which are directed towards the good of the whole body. Ministers who are endowed with sacred power are at the service of their brothers and sisters, so that all who belong to the people of God, and therefore enjoy real Christian dignity, by cooperating with each other freely and in an orderly manner in pursuit of the same goal, may attain salvation.[25]

It must not be assumed that "sacred power" is limited to those in ordained ministries. The council made it clear that all of the faithful participate in the threefold *munera Christi* (Christ's priestly, prophetic, and royal function):

[The laity,] that is to say, the faithful who, since they have been incorporated into Christ by baptism, constitute the people of God and, in their own way participate in Christ's priestly, prophetic and royal function, exercise their own role in the mission of the whole Christian people in the church and in the world.[26]

The present canonical posture, which restricts lay participation in the power of governance to "cooperation in its exercise,"[27] is purely positive ecclesiastical law, not an intrinsic limitation or a matter of "divine law." There is ample theological warrant and historical precedent for the possession and use of the power of governance by laypersons.

The principle of subsidiary function is firmly embedded in Catholic social teaching, and its application within the church has been reiterated by its highest authorities. Subsidiarity should be a basic principle of the exercise of authority in the church.

Pope John Paul II restated the principle in his encyclical *Centesimus annus*:

Here again the principle of subsidiarity must be respected: A community of a higher order should not interfere in the internal life of a community of a lower order, depriving the latter of its functions, but rather support it in case of need and help to coordinate its activity with the activities of the rest of society, always with a view to the common good.[28]

The principles that guided the revision of the *Code of Canon Law*, approved by the Episcopal Synod of 1967 and included in the preface of the 1983 code, contain one which urges the greater application of the principle of subsidiarity.[29]

The principle must be respected and applied in parishes and other local communities and institutions in their relationships with the diocese. Subsidiarity implies that local churches exercise appropriate self-direction and initiative. It does not imply their complete autonomy or aloof independence; after all they are all in close communion. But dioceses really exist to support, assist, coordinate, and supplement the activities of parishes, not the other way around.

American cultural expectations about the exercise of authority should also be taken into consideration in its use within the church. For example, a sense of fundamental fairness is basic to the American way of thinking. Special privilege and unequal treatment are viewed with suspicion and distaste. On the other hand, a sense of compassion and mercy far outweighs a harsh, exacting, inflexible justice. Reconciliation and inclusion are valued above alienation and exclusion. Measured, considered actions are vastly preferred to those which appear hasty, ill-considered, or abrupt.

Finally, the church requires good order. Those in authority and those subject to authority are both responsible for that order. The apostle Paul said that chaos and confusion were not acceptable. "If the whole church meets in one place and everyone speaks in tongues," if outsiders should come in, "will they not say you are out of your minds?" "Everything should be done for building up," Paul wrote about the public use of the Spirit's gifts. "Everything must be done properly and in good order" because "God is not a God of disorder, but of peace" (1 Cor 14:23, 26, 40, 33).

The lingering questions with regard to discipline in the church are how close an order is required, how differently can Catholics and their communities act and still remain in communion? The outside parameters of an answer to those questions are found in the ancient saying that John XXIII was fond of repeating: "In necessary things unity, in doubtful matters freedom, and in all things charity."

Notes

[1] 1983 *Code of Canon Law,* canon 135.

[2] *DH* 2-4, 8, 10-12; *GS* 16-17, 41.

[3] See, for example, J. Dallen, *The Reconciling Community: The Rite of Penance* (New York: Pueblo, 1986), 56-99.

[4] *Canon Law Digest*, v. 2, 146; v. 3, 377-79.

[5] *Rite of Penance*, December 2, 1973, pars. 60-66.

[6] For example, see R. Page, "L'absolution collective au Canada," *Studia Canonica* 29:2 (1995), 493-508.

[7] T. Ventura, "Old Wine in New Wineskins," *Chicago Studies* 34:2 (August 1995), 111; this article is the main source for this case.

[8] Ibid., 112.

[9] Ibid., 120.

[10] Ibid., 121.

[11] Ibid., 122.

[12] Ibid. A postscript to this "confrontation" appeared in the St. Cletus, LaGrange, Illinois, parish bulletin on November 26, 1996, after Bernardin's death:

> A couple of years ago many pastors were put upon by Archdiocesan authorities regarding our general confession services. We were informed that perhaps they weren't necessary. We believed they were. We decided to continue having them. I wrote an article in this space that explained why.
>
> Someone sent the article in, and I received a letter from the Cardinal some days later. In it, he reminded me that the Church as an organization needs certain disciplines, and that, as a pastor, it would be good to remember that we all can't just do whatever we want to.
>
> Some weeks later I saw him, and I told him I had received his note. He told me then that making decisions and following up on them was an important part of the pastorate. But then he told me that writing about them sometimes and putting them in print was another story. He cautioned me as to the difference between doing something and writing about it. I understood. I will always credit him first, in my own mind, with prudence (quoted in *Cristifidelis* 15:1 [Lent 1997] 4).

It is instructive to recall a historical parallel in the development of the sacrament of penance. When monastic or "tariff" penance (the precursor to the later standard form of private confession) began to replace canonical penance in the early middle ages, church authorities condemned and outlawed it. The newer form thrived in spite of this opposition (Dallen, *The Reconciling Community*, 100-38).

[13] The paper was published as an article in *The Jurist* 29:4 (October 1969), 228-38.

[14] *Origins* 2 (October 12, 1972), 254.

[15] *Origins* 2 (July 27, 1972), 130–36.

[16] *Origins* 2 (September 7, 1972), 176-77. Bishop Tracy's response to Krol's announcement was twofold. On August 18 he expressed "delight" at the development and said that "our diocese stands ready . . . to follow current discipline in the matter while awaiting its final disposition from Rome." And on August 25 he stated that "the Diocese of Baton Rouge has adopted a policy of propriety whereby no further statements . . . will be made pending the outcome of the study . . . which naturally will consider on the one hand, the sanctity and indissolubility of Christian marriage, and on the other hand the plight of certain individuals who find themselves in good conscience situations" (ibid., 177).

[17] CDF Prot. Nos. 1284/66, 139/69.

[18] CDF Prot. No. 1284/66.

[19] J. Provost, "Intolerable Marriage Situations Revisited," *The Jurist* 40:1 (1980), 176–77. There have been several important developments related to this pastoral problem in the intervening years, but the basic situation of diverse pastoral practices in the United States has not changed much. Cf. K. Himes and J. Coriden, "Pastoral Care of the Divorced and Remarried," *Theological Studies* 57 (1996), 97–123.

[20] This case too is real; however, since it was not publicized, names and circumstances have been changed to protect those involved.

[21] Weber contrasted coercive "power" with legitimate "authority" and distinguished authority into three forms depending on its source: traditional, charismatic, and rational or legal.

[22] "All authority in heaven and earth has been given to me" (Mt 28:18).

[23] "You will receive power when the Holy Spirit has come upon you; and you will be my witnesses . . . to the ends of the earth" (Acts 1:8).

[24] In Mark and Matthew Jesus' saying on authority is placed after the bold request by the brothers James and John for places of special favor in Jesus' future kingdom. When the other ten heard of their request they became indignant.

Jesus called them and said to them, "You know that among the Gentiles those whom they recognize as their rulers lord it over them, and their great ones are tyrants over them. But it is not so among you; but whoever wishes to become great among you must be your servant, and whoever wishes to be first among you must be the slave of all. For the Son of Man came not to be served but to serve and to give his life a ransom for many" (Mk 10:42–45; parallels: Mt 20:25–28; Lk 22:24–27; Jn 13:2–15).

[25] *LG* 18; parallels: 20, 24, and 27.

[26] *LG* 31; see also 7, 12, 33–37, and *AA* 1–3.

[27] Canon 129 of the 1983 *Code* stated that those in sacred orders are capable *(habiles)* of power while laypersons *cooperari possum in exercitio potestatis*.

[28] May 1, 1991, *AAS* 83 (1991), 854. Pius XI, in *Quadragesimo anno*, May 15, 1931, called it "that most weighty principle, which cannot be set aside or changed [and which] remains fixed and unshaken in social philosophy" (par. 79, *AAS* 23 [1931] 203). John XXIII repeated the definition of the "guiding principle" in *Mater et magistra*, May 15, 1961 *(AAS* 53 [1961], 414). Pius XII (address *AAS* 38 [1946], 145) and Paul VI (allocution, October 27, 1969, *AAS* 61 [1969], 729) affirmed the application of the principle within the church.

[29] *Communicationes* 1 (1969), 80–82; *Codex Iuris Canonici Fontium Annotatione Auctus* (1989), xxv.

4

AUTHORITY IN AMERICA

Philip Selznick

In American history distrust of authority has been a lively passion and a beguiling heritage. This was a nation "conceived in liberty" and born in rebellion from established authority. A century of Western migration, a pioneering ethos; industrial revolution; urbanization; extension of democracy—all produced an unruly culture, individualist, pluralist, careless of tradition, unburdened by a feudal past. For Americans, "the state" became an alien expression, not suited to a democratic people, inconsistent with the moral, economic, and political primacy of civil society. A strong commitment to the federal principle, which understands the nation as a unity of unities, together with constitutional provisions for separation of powers, accustomed the people to divided sovereignty and to periods of divided government as well. This repudiation of a unitary state has had fateful consequences for the claims of authority in American political institutions.

And yet, even as exuberant individualism progressed, Americans could find comfort in a fairly stable world of kinship and community. These anchors demanded responsibility and enforced conformity. They also made possible the non-conformity of greatness, as in the lives of Abraham Lincoln, Frank Lloyd Wright, Thomas Edison, and many other American "originals." In effect, an infrastructure of authority—mainly intimate and person-centered—served as a kind of social capital able to energize as well as temper the forces that were creating modern America.

The special features of American history have been overtaken and exacerbated by the more general forces of modernization, especially urbanization, secularization, and rationalization. These trends have brought about a separation of spheres, especially household and work, religion and community, education and parenting. They have produced a pervasive weakening of traditional social bonds. New unities have been substituted, based on more impersonal, more fragile, more fragmented ways of acting and belonging. Today the main forms of social participation are segmental and tentative, governed by an imagery of contract and a preference for limited obligation. In such a world, ideals of commitment lose their hold on the moral imagination.

The specific patterns are familiar to all. They include the decline of kinship as a source of obligation and as a resource for apprenticeship and occupational choice; the rise of the detached nuclear family and the fragmentation of life within it; the entry of women into the labor force, in unprecedented numbers and within all social classes, in part supported by new feminist ideologies; the sexual revolution, especially the widely condoned separation of sex and marriage; the increasing insecurity of employment as corporate leaders become more single-minded in their pursuit of short-run gains.

A major outcome is the erosion of parental, religious, and political authority. In all these areas we see a substantial waning of loyalty and obedience. Americans have never been comfortable with subordination, but the spirit of modernity makes subordination especially difficult to accept. An egalitarian temper, suspicious of all elites, saps the self-confidence of leaders and institutions. Authority becomes inherently unstable, anxious, and placative.

Something special should be said about the egalitarian temptation to regard hierarchy and inequality as inherently evil. This leads to an anti-elitist ideology that discounts the indispensable role of elites in many spheres of life, including science, education, art, religion, and politics. Although some kinds of elites are merely privileged holders of power or wealth, others nurture important skills, standards, and ideals. Many values are precarious, subject to erosion and distortion, especially under pressure for quick returns. Democracy itself depends on the effective functioning of legal and political elites. Freedom of speech and association are not self-sustaining. They require "eternal vigilance," which is mainly the work of committed elites. Democracy presumes responsive government, but responsiveness degenerates and undermines government when citizen participation overwhelms the process and officials flee from making judgments.

The Union of Trust and Criticism

The great question is this: Can we counter the drift toward a disabling anomie—the downside of distrust—without giving up the spirit of criticism? Can we do so without forgetting Jefferson's dictum that freedom is founded "in jealousy, and not in confidence; it is jealousy, not confidence, which prescribes limited constitutions, to bind down those whom we are obliged to trust with power." Much depends on how we understand authority. If attitudes toward authority are complex and ambivalent, this is at least partly due to the variety of its meanings and the subtlety of its claims.

A threshold meaning is fairly widely accepted: authority is a rightful claim to deference or obedience. The criterion of rightfulness distinguishes authority from power, and that is the beginning of wisdom.

But rightfulness takes many forms. Directives may be accepted as rightful even if that acceptance is deeply flawed in mind and spirit, that is, in the quality of consent. When consent is supine, coerced, or uncritical, what is rightful remains an unanswered question.

It is important to distinguish the right to hold office from the legitimacy of specific decisions. The right to hold office when duly appointed or elected may be largely unquestioned, but the extent of the officeholder's authority may be hotly contested, as in criticism of the federal judiciary; or of the president's authority as commander-in-chief; or the authority of corporate officials to spend money for philanthropy, or for bribes. Indeed most questioning of authority has to do with the way it is exercised, not with the initial grant or premise. Authority is fully legitimate only if it is exercised in rightful ways, within rightful limits. Thus understood, authority is forever problematic and subject to scrutiny.

There is, of course, a close connection between "gross" legitimacy and legitimacy "in depth." The former is eroded when specific decisions show evidence of folly, corruption, or oppression. This was the logic of the Declaration of Independence: "Prudence, indeed, will dictate that governments long established should not be changed for light and transient causes. . . . But when a long train of abuses . . . " In our time the trauma of Vietnam undermined the authority of foreign-policy "experts," and of the U.S. government as well.

The root source of ambivalence in attitudes toward authority is the menace of domination. Domination is the negative *telos* of authority, captured by Lord Acton's famous remark that "power tends to corrupt and absolute power corrupts absolutely." The American experience has built upon this truth, creating institutions wary of this natural propensity for authority to become a springboard to domination.

This critical posture can sometimes do more harm than good. To remain healthy and beneficial, such criticism must take place within a framework of trust and commitment. Faith in democracy, in the efficacy of government, and in the virtues of rule of law, in freedom of speech, freedom of worship, parental responsibility, free enterprise, separation of church and state—these are among the shared premises that make criticism coherent and self-preserving.

The alternative is a general attitude of distrust and deconstruction. This was the posture of classical Marxism, which stigmatized modern values and institutions as irredeemably "bourgeois" and therefore without moral worth. We meet it again in postmodern criticisms of liberal and traditional society.

So authority is about limits—limits that apply in different ways to rulers and ruled, officials and citizens. Thus the rule of law requires, in the first instance, systematic control of official discretion. The same ideal also requires a broader culture of lawfulness, which includes deference to legitimate authority and self-restraint in the pursuit of private interests.

Acting within limits, and accepting subordination, is not a wholly negative experience. People can be more autonomous as well as effective when choice is informed by moral discipline. Deference to authority liberates as it constrains insofar as we gain energy and confidence from authoritative ways of thinking and acting. In many contexts choice can be a debilitating burden. When people are guided by recognized rules and principles they can focus on what they do best; they can gain from the competence of others; and the experience of belonging to a well-ordered community is a reliable source of security and empowerment.

AUTHORITARIAN VS. AUTHORITATIVE

It is a sign of our resistance to the positive, life-enhancing aspects of authority that we do not have good expressions for distinguishing authoritarian regimes from groups governed by wholesome norms of deference, commitment, and self-restraint. As usually understood in contemporary thought, an authoritarian regime is autocratic, even despotic, but not totalitarian. Authoritarian systems privilege the wishes of rulers or commanders. They may act arbitrarily and run roughshod over the needs of subordinate individuals and groups. Their reach is limited, however. A totalitarian regime can be more ambitious. It seeks to control, and is able to control, all or most of social life.

An authoritative order—perhaps someone will suggest a better locution—is neither authoritarian nor totalitarian. Rather, it is a system governed by widespread respect—among the rulers and the ruled—for shared values, purposes, and institutions, including institutions that represent legitimate authority.

This respect for an objective order is what the great sociologist Max Weber had in mind when he distinguished "rational-legal" authority from "traditional" and "charismatic" authority. These modes of ordering—these roads to legitimacy—may be more interdependent than Weber supposed. An objective order is not necessarily impersonal or "rational-legal." Fidelity to values and loyalty to an institution are often enhanced if authority is personalized; that is, made vivid in the lives of particular parents, judges, clerics, or leaders whose individual qualities embody and express appropriate virtues. The most effective systems of authority combine traditional, charismatic, and rational-legal principles. Weber's analytical distinctions should not be read as precluding, or as invitations to ignore, the empirical and moral continuities. Person-centered trust has a vital part to play in sustaining the authority of abstract ideas.

A Paradigm—The American Common-Law Tradition

The most instructive paradigm for the union of trust and criticism is the American version of the common-law tradition.

That tradition includes judicial review of statutes and of administrative decisions, and the concept of a "living" or "evolving" Constitution.

Perhaps the most remarkable feature of the common-law tradition is its openness to criticism and reconstruction. This judge-made law differs significantly from ordinary legislation. It is not supposed to be an assertion of political will. Rather, it is a product of sustained inquiry into the principles that constitute a legal heritage and how those principles should be adapted to specific needs and circumstances. As a result, the common law is always open to revision. Furthermore, rules and precedents have variable authority. Some are more firmly grounded than others in statutory language, in persuasive argument, in social practice. This variability has a crucial significance: it offers leverage for criticism. Lawyers are invited to test the authority of a purportedly governing rule or precedent.

This practice finds much support in the prominence we give to partisan advocacy. Self-help and self-assertion are mainstays of the common-law tradition. In their pursuit of justice the parties are expected to take the initiative and to exercise wide-ranging responsibility for presenting proofs and arguments. The debate is about facts, but also about the meaning and relevance of legal rules, principles, and concepts.

This culture of argument is manifest in the published opinions—including concurrences and dissents—of appellate judges. The opinion makes the reasoning available to scrutiny, and dissents testify to the problematic authority of judicial reasoning and the potential for change in the light of fresh thought and new circumstances.

All this takes place within a framework of accepted tradition. The basic legitimacy of that tradition remains immense despite the prevalence of robust debate.

Much the same may be said of constitutional interpretation where the ethos of criticism is strong and stirs much political controversy. But acceptance of the Constitution is not eroded.

Although the decisions of judges are often condemned, the institution of judicial review is not in danger. Respect for the Constitution is profoundly traditional, insensibly absorbed, without debate, by successive generations of Americans.

SCIENCE

A beneficial union of trust and criticism is by no means confined to our legal tradition. A fairly obvious example is the ethos and practice of science. In science no idea is beyond criticism; every finding and every theory is subject to correction. Nevertheless, each inquiry must begin from a point already laid down. Much must be taken as given, and as authoritative. These received materials are substantive as well as methodological; they empower and liberate the mind of the scientist. They can also be unduly confining, but the remedy is more sophistication and better science, not pseudo-science. In America a passion for invention and for resistance to authority may have brought an added measure of energy and imagination to the scientific community.

More generally, the world of scholarship and teaching, at its best, displays a special fidelity to the union of trust and criticism. We want students to be free and creative; we expect them to push forward the frontiers of scholarship. At the same time we must do our part to provide them with a furnished mind. To do so we must win their trust. We might like their admiration, but we settle for respect. Some of us demand fairly intense socialization into the thoughtways of a discipline, and this too can confine as well as empower.

FAMILY

Most of us would agree that a healthy family—or a healthy friendship—must be capable of sustaining both trust and criticism. We may believe in the importance of parental authority, but we do not suppose that such authority is properly despotic, indifferent to context, or insensitive to the changing needs of children, as they mature, for independence and self-definition. Managing this tension is, of course, the master problem of parental authority.

EMPLOYMENT

In American industry the need for a union of trust and criticism is dimly perceived and difficult to establish. Yet it has been widely discussed, at least implicitly. Drawing on a reservoir of respect for property, Americans have been all too ready to accept the legitimacy of top-down management: "I run this business because I own it." However, top-down management has been much criticized, and to some extent reformed, in the interests of productivity, initiative, morale, and commitment. The quest is for greater flexibility and creativity, which require better communication and consultation at all levels. For this alternative to work, the enterprise needs an organizational culture of trust, community, and legitimated criticism. In such a culture people are protected from arbitrary treatment, including unjustified layoffs and dismissals; supervision is supportive, not rigid, intrusive, and mistrustful. A morality of cooperation prevails.

ISSUES OF TRADITION AND MODERNITY

Each of these examples—law, science, family, employment—gives a distinctive shape to the union of trust and criticism. At the same time, each speaks in its own way to broader issues of tradition and modernity.

We cannot do without tradition, which reflects the human need for cultural premises and the social reality of tacit knowledge. Émile Durkheim once said that "a society without prejudices [prejudgments] would resemble an organism without reflexes." Indeed all enduring communities, all enduring institutions, encourage fidelity to appropriate traditions. They also invent some, if necessary.

Nevertheless, tradition is understood and experienced in different ways. It may be thought of as a body of specific commandments to think and act certain ways, without reflection, in a spirit of exigent and perhaps redemptive conformity. A different vision of what tradition consists of and what it requires brings to mind fundamental principles as well as specific rules or rites. Principles underpin rules and justify them. They are also tools for criticizing rules, and for changing them. Thus understood, tradition is the parent and friend—not the enemy—of reflective morality.

The upshot is a point of view we may call *critical affirmation*. It is affirmative in that it embraces moral, cultural, and institutional premises; critical in its demand for reasoned elaboration of those premises and for testing the rightness of policies and decisions. Critical affirmation is a hallmark of American culture, at least when the latter is seen in its best light.

Critical affirmation is a potent but unstable blend of confidence and skepticism. Americans created, in many ways, a culture of confidence. Yet our institutions have been skeptical as well. Although the Declaration of Independence exuded confidence, the Constitution conveyed a more nuanced message. Its provisions spoke to the need for balance and order, continuity of tradition, strong government, and limited powers. The Constitution did much to form the nation's character and identity. But it could not produce an austere and disciplined polity. More was done to release energies than to contain them. In a setting of restless striving and open frontiers, the American political community became notably confident, and more exuberantly democratic than stoically republican.

THE COSTS OF SOPHISTICATION

Can this healthy-minded spirit of critical affirmation be sustained? Can authority be trusted as well as questioned? These are big issues. The answers may be beyond our reach, contingent on forces we can neither foresee nor control. It may be helpful, however, to review some words of doctrine that jeopardize the fragile union of trust and criticism. These may be understood as costs of sophistication. They are the weaknesses of our strengths and the humbling defects of our virtues. They also have special relevance to us as intellectuals and teachers.

Plurality and Relativism

The modern temper has encouraged appreciation for different ways of life and different roads to moral truth. For a time this expressed basic confidence in truth, including the truth that all people (and peoples) have a prima-facie claim to respect and self-determination. More recently the celebration of plurality has become more passionate and less optimistic. As a radical relativism has taken hold, the very idea of truth—especially moral truth—is challenged. Furthermore, the same passion is expressed in rampant multiculturalism, which weakens the authority of more comprehensive unities. This is very different from the pluralism we associate with doctrines of subsidiarity and what James Madison called "the federal principle." Those doctrines are self-limiting, whereas multiculturalism is not.

Indeterminacy and Absolutism

It is a frustrating paradox that knowledge and sophistication bring in their train a loss of certainty. We become more aware of contingency; of relevant variables; of the diverse and subtle values at stake in family life, education, and the administration of justice. Indeed, the richer our understanding of reason—especially how it differs from rationalism—the more sensitive we become to the pull of indeterminacy.

We have seen that critical affirmation, as a way of experiencing authority, is drawn toward generalization. The tendency is to place faith in abstract ideas, such as moral equality, which are open to interpretation and therefore to criticism. When we must deal with a policy issue, such as affirmative action, we know that the ideal of moral equality is relevant, but we differ about its meaning and therefore about its authority as a guide to judgment. The "proposition," as Lincoln put it, "that all men are created equal" is not empty rhetoric, but it is indeterminate and contested.

It has been difficult for people to accept the pragmatist view, as expressed by John Dewey, that uncertainty is no bar to truth, if truth is understood as necessarily contingent and subject to correction. One response is the postmodern fascination with indeterminacy and deconstruction, as if the world is readily dissolved in a sea of subjectivity. A different, no-less-dangerous response seeks to escape uncertainty by embracing rigid and unchangeable conceptions of rights, duties, and authority.

The Sovereignty of Will

Modernity's greatest challenge to morality is a sensed sovereignty of will. Autonomy and choice are leitmotifs of modernity. Man makes himself, it is said, and this includes the moral order. Morality is made, not discovered. Hence will, not knowledge, takes center stage. In modern democracy the "will of the people" is celebrated, but there is no answer to the question, how is the will of the people to be governed?

The American experience has been an answer of sorts: the will of the people is constrained by the Constitution. Much depends, however, on the degree to which the Constitution is invested with moral authority, as a framework within which freedom is limited as well as guaranteed. It should help us to see that will is not sovereign but rather transcended by requirements of participation in a moral order we can and must interpret, but cannot make. To serve this need, the Constitution must be understood as incorporating principles of justice, as well as claims of reason and those of a distinctive heritage. If we nurture this idea, we can improve the prospects for authority in America.

5

PANEL DISCUSSION

*James Coriden, Avery Dulles, Joseph Komonchak,
and Philip Selznick*

INTRODUCTION

ROBERT IMBELLI: I should begin with hearty thanks to those
who prepared the papers, Fathers Avery Dulles of Fordham
University, James Coriden of the Washington Theological
Union, Joseph Komonchak of Catholic University, and our
special guest, Professor Philip Selznick. They have really provided a service to all of us.

What we asked each of the writers to do in preparation for
this discussion, at least the three who prepared explicitly on
ecclesial authority, was the following.

We asked them to look over their papers again and to lift
up from their own paper an issue or concern that in some ways
was central to their presentation. So, not to do a resumé of the
paper, which we have all read, but on a second glance, to say
what they find there as being a particular concern to them.
Second, in the spirit of common ground, what legitimate concern have they read or heard so far that is not represented in

their own paper? And finally, what sort of assessment of the cultural or ecclesial situation may be implicit in their paper?

It is an attempt to ask them to do something of what Augustine called a *retractatio*, a relooking at something they had written earlier in the light of further developments. Each person of the three will make a presentation trying to touch those issues. That will be followed by each of the other two raising questions of agreement or disagreement, and then by a brief response on the part of the original presenter.

At the end of this first session Professor Philip Selznick will give us a reading of what he has heard from his perspective. We hope thereby to do justice to the papers and to allow for some second thoughts, but also to begin to serve the purpose of the whole conference by clarifying some issues that we may want to pursue. So, with that, Father Dulles will begin.

AVERY DULLES

AVERY DULLES: This will be a *retractatio* only in the Augustinian sense of the word and not a retraction in the modern sense. Although I may have to retract something by the end, I'm not going to go about it so soon.

One of the things that runs through my paper and underlies it is a somewhat sharp distinction in principle between sacred and secular society and authority. It seems to me in secular society the structures of government are set up from below by the people in order to meet certain set needs. Whereas in the sacred order, it is God who intervenes in history to institute and reveal a way of salvation, and God sets up a structured community, with sacramental structures if you like, to preserve and transmit the revelation and to bring about this salvific dispensation.

The church, as I see it, was founded on Peter and the apostles, who have a divine commission and a promise of God's presence with them to abide throughout the rest of history. So, I think in the church the hierarchical principle is very important and has to be safeguarded. I don't know exactly how to define this hierarchical principle, but it seems to me the plenitude of power is vested in a single body that perpetuates itself by cooption. That does not mean that there are not initiatives from below. Of course, there are. The Spirit is given to the whole church and initiatives come about wherever the Spirit is active; the governing body has to discern the presence of the Spirit and validate it. It may sometimes make mistakes, but it nevertheless has that responsibility.

Now, when it comes to making decisions, the governing body that has the doctrinal authority may want to conduct consultations. I think it's very important that the consultations not take the form of pressure of any kind because the decision has to be made freely in the light of revelation which comes down through scripture and tradition and is studied in a prayerful way to apply to what may be a new situation. And for those who are consulted, it is important that they themselves be immersed in the tradition and operate according to the criteria proper to the church.

Now, on these questions that I dealt with in the paper—the birth-control decision and the ordination of women—there was a certain consultation process in each case. But I think it is important that when one does consult, if one is announcing a formal consultation, it should be about a question that is genuinely open. Otherwise expectations are aroused that are very difficult to quiet.

I think the really open question on the birth-control commission was whether the pill constituted a legitimate application of the principle of intercourse during the so-called safe periods. It somehow got expanded into a larger question of whether to reverse the traditional teaching of the church in the encyclical of Pius XI and so forth. I don't know how it got expanded to that point. But then expectations were created that were very difficult to quiet down later.

And finally, with the ordination of women, I don't think there was a formal consultation. There was, of course, the 1976 declaration of the Congregation for the Doctrine of the Faith, which was a study commissioned by Paul VI, but there was not an open consultation on that point.

However, I think what was failing, maybe, was the degree of trust in the magisterial authority until it should issue a clearly infallible declaration. I think it is unfortunate if the absence of trust in the church gets to the point where nothing will solve the question other than an infallible pronouncement. You shouldn't have to use nuclear weapons in every case. I think there should be more habitual trust in the teaching of magisterial authority, even when it is not on the very highest level, and I think that fits in very well with the quotation that Father Komonchak has from John Henry Newman. That's about what I wanted to say.

JAMES CORIDEN: This is difficult because Avery, I think, had by far the best paper, the most cogently and clearly presented. But let me just ask two questions that I take to be differences in ecclesiological assumptions lying behind some of your assertions, Avery.

As I finished reading the paper, I said we're back into the separation of *ecclesia discens* (the teaching church) and *ecclesia docens* (the learning church). Those are old categories and very familiar to you, but the impression given in your paper is that we had gone back into a separation of the teaching church from the learning church; that the presence of the Spirit is mainly in the officeholders and is only in exceptional circumstances located or given hearing and voice elsewhere. And it seems to me that we have a long history of revisions of serious teachings, not infallible but serious teachings, on matters like usury and slavery and war and the exploitation of the earth that indicate that all wisdom or assistance from the Spirit to the church is not in officeholders. That's one question.

And the second is, Do the convictions and practices of the faithful constitute a theologically significant evidence of reception? That is to say, are they really manifestations of God's

Spirit working in the church, or are they reflections of the secular mentality or the local culture?

Related to that, when is it harmful to let a debate run its course in the confident expectation that a consensus will develop around the truth? If those in authority are not ready to say something, then nothing should be said.

JOSEPH KOMONCHAK: I have a couple of general remarks. This is more background. It seems to me that part of the problem to which your paper is addressed, Avery, is that in the final moment in each of these two cases it appears that it was the pope alone who was settling the issue. This is to some degree a problem. It is particularly so after the experience that the whole church had of the Second Vatican Council, which was an exercise of the highest level of church authority, but one which was collegial and in that sense collective from the beginning.

And in that context of recalling the council, I do think that one of the things that affects us, or at least, as they say, those of us who are of a certain age, is the memory of exercises of authority before the council where we had, in a sense, two generations of suspicious attitudes on the part of highest authority in Rome toward movements of renewal and toward some of the pioneers of them, resulting often in quite unjust measures taken against them.

So there did develop a certain culture of suspicion within the church, so that when some people hear a new document has come from Rome, their first question is to say, "Oh, my God, how bad is it?" This is for me evidence of a real crisis in authority, because it is the opposite of trust. That is simply sort of a contextual statement, but it does raise this issue: To what degree did, in fact, collegial conversation or consultation, even simply at the level of consultation with the bishops, enter into the two judgments that you reviewed? And then the larger question is: To what degree should it?

I wonder also whether, if we sat down—and I know it is not our purpose to investigate each of these things in detail—whether the two cases, that of contraception and that of the ordination of women, don't have some significant differences that would alter one's perceptions—the one, *Humanae vitae*, claiming a natural-law basis; the other having to do with the constitution of the church—and decisions on the two issues having different consequences for the life of the church and for the life of particular individuals.

You admit that perhaps you are stating things somewhat too crudely when you say that the division is between conservatives and progressives, or between the sacral and the secular spirit. I do think that that may be prejudicing the issue from the beginning, because many of the people who have found difficulties with either of the two positions did so on what they thought at least were not simply secular grounds but specifically Christian and theological grounds. So, those are my two comments.

AVERY DULLES: Well, with regard to the distinction between the *ecclesia discens* and *docens*, I think Vatican II reaffirmed that in saying that those who teach authoritatively for the church are the pope and the bishops. That's in *Lumen gentium* 25 quite clearly, that theologians and others can be teachers *in* the church, but they do not *teach* the church and they don't have any authoritative teaching power. They cannot constitute doctrine by themselves but only recommend it or propose it. So, I think it is important to keep a distinction there. That certainly does not mean that the Spirit is restricted to the official teachers, the hierarchical teachers. I think, as I said in my introductory remarks, the Spirit can work wherever he, or she if you like, pleases throughout the Body of Christ or even beyond the Body of Christ so that the Spirit works—blows where it wills—and not all wisdom is reposed in the hierarchy. Nevertheless, they have a specific function within the church that they cannot neglect or palm off on others, though not all wisdom is in the officeholders.

With regard to the practices of the faithful, yes, they may be a sign of the presence of the Spirit or they may come from a different spirit. Therefore, they have to be discerned. And I think the discernment ultimately is the responsibility of the hierarchical leadership, assisted by others, of course.

And as for the debate running its course, sometimes the debate does lead to a consensus, but very often the debate, far from leading to a consensus, leads to a hardening of positions in which people become antagonistically opposed to one another. And I think on the particular questions that my paper dealt with, the debate was not leading toward a consensus at all but rather in the opposite direction. So, I don't think that letting the debate run its course would have led to a consensus at all. That's my own opinion on the matter, which has no particular authority, of course.

As for the remarks by Father Komonchak, certainly the council itself is a collegial exercise of hierarchical authority, but that doesn't mean that it always has to be done in a formally collegial manner. That is very plain, I think, in *Lumen gentium* itself and the *Nota Praevia,* to which I referred also, so that the pope does have the authority to decide questions without formal consultation of the bishops and a strictly collegial action. I think that's exactly what happened in the two cases that I studied.

But there is a certain culture of suspicion toward Rome. It is certainly a fact. I think it's partly due to the interpretation of Vatican II. There was a tendency to interpret it as a reversal of everything that had gone on in the fifty years before rather than as a development. But really, I don't think that the shift from, let's say, Pius XI or Pius XII to the council is all that great. I think it's more a nuancing of what had been previously taught, and the opposition has been somewhat exaggerated, generating a climate of suspicion as though the pontificate of Pius XII was simply the dark ages. I think in many ways that pontificate led up to the council and prepared for it.

There were, of course, certain problems and questions raised, and there may have been some mistakes made, especially, I think, in the application of *Humani generis*. I think the document *Humani generis* can be defended, but it was rather ruthlessly applied by the generals of the Jesuits and the Dominicans and perhaps some other people. So that did generate this climate of suspicion.

The two cases are quite diverse, I grant, in their application to the life of the faithful, because most of the faithful are not applicants for ordination. It affects only a small number, whereas contraception affects very many people in the church.

And the last point—the sacral versus the secular. That terminology, like conservative and liberal, is always a little too crude. Sometimes labels like that are a little helpful, but they always have to be nuanced. And I grant you that many people who were favoring a change of doctrine in those two cases had what they considered to be Christian warrants for it. But I think on the whole they were also saying that they were learning from the movement of secular culture. I said in my paper that there are many things that we do learn and should learn from secular progress. So, I'm not writing that off by any means.

JOSEPH KOMONCHAK

JOSEPH KOMONCHAK: In my brief comments here I'm not going to refer to the two pastoral letters that provided the take-off point for my reflections, but we were asked to focus on a few things that were in our minds, and these remarks have to do more with the section in which I offer some reflections on the question.

One of my main concerns was to try to articulate the limited effectiveness of simple appeals to formal or de iure office or authority; that is, that it is enough to insist that a particular enactment, whether a law or a teaching, comes from an authorized person or office. This I think is dangerous even in the case of law, but it's even more problematic in the case of teaching. Here you enter into the whole question of the voluntaristic versus rationalistic or intellectualistic understanding of law, and so on, which I think has had some consequences in the theology of the magisterium over the last two or three centuries.

And I approached the issue by considering exercises of effective authority; that is, instances in which authority works—where, I believe, the prior attitudes of those under authority and their free and intelligent response to a particular exercise enter into the very constitution of the authority relationship. So, my argument is to some degree that authority doesn't exist by itself, but that authority is always a social relationship, and that constitutive of it is the attitude of those who are considered to be under the authority.

Therefore, the absence of these responses and characteristics and attitudes in those under authority indicates that the persons in authority have lost authority, either completely or for the moment. That yields a kind of a definition of authority as acknowledged and anticipated trustworthiness.

I want to argue that a successful exercise of authority, whether elsewhere or in the church, is not in itself necessarily a parade or demonstration of the reasons for a position, but rather that it succeeds because others believe or trust that good reasons do lie behind the teaching. In the other article that I submitted,[1] there is a footnote that refers to Carl J. Friedrich's definition of authority as "a capacity for reasoned deliberation on the basis of common values." I do think that that enters into this question. I think one difference between myself and the other two here is that they may emphasize more than I do the differences between authority as exercised in the church and as exercised elsewhere.

A second point is that my paper suggests attention to the conditions, personal and ecclesial, for successful, that is effective, exercises of authority. First, on the part of those in authority, so that people are not placed in offices that ought to be trusted who cannot be trusted. Second, on the part of those under authority, so that they also acknowledge the legitimacy of authority and are themselves ready to trust it.

Those are two different ways of saying that both parties need to be converted and that authority cannot substitute for conversion. So, I have a brief and somewhat gnomic comment there that some authorities who ought to be trusted are not in fact trusted, and some authorities who ought not be trusted are, in fact, trusted. It seems to me that you're not going to settle that issue by stamping your foot in a defense of purely formal authority.

The larger issue is the one suggested by my first quotation from Newman, where he talks about the prior necessity of admiration, trust, and love for Christ and his church, without which you are not really going to be able seriously to approach questions of authority. That is, it seems to me, also a precondition for effective authority.

We were asked to come up with some obvious objections to our positions. I had to struggle, of course, but I came up with two. The first one, Am I not reducing de iure authority to effective authority? And two, Who decides whether an enactment is reasonable?

With regard to the first, in modern social science there has been a shift from a normative notion of legitimacy in the past to an empirical notion in which an authority is often said to be legitimate simply if it, in fact, is successful.

Now, that more empirical notion of legitimacy, it seems to me, has some analytical usefulness. Obviously, it is appropriate in trying to decide—well, you may make all kinds of claims for the authority of the law or of the teaching—but then you also are going to be able to measure this by finding out, in fact, how many people are obeying the law or agreeing with the teaching.

But the modern notion does not settle whether the enactment or the response to it was appropriate or reasonable, and

I think that question remains. All you have to do is look, for example, at laws which once in our country prohibited interracial marriages or required forced sterilizations. These are laws that came from the appropriate legal authority, but one can ask whether they are legitimate by some other criteria. Those questions remain, and I do not intend by my analysis to reduce the question of genuine authority to the question of whether it in fact has been received.

The same thing could apply in the church as well. In some of the examples that Jim Coriden mentions there are exercises of authority. You can consider the Pontifical Biblical Institute at one point prohibiting Catholics from maintaining that a certain verse in the First Epistle of John did not belong to the original text. That kind of thing. The question will remain, Is that a legitimate exercise of authority?

On the question of who decides whether an enactment is reasonable, that of course is a question that still troubles us in the United States, where the Supreme Court in a couple of cases has in effect said it is not up to the citizens to decide whether a law is reasonable or not. One clear example is the exclusion by the Supreme Court of any kind of right to selective conscientious objection. That, it seems to me, is an issue that in part rests upon a fear that if you leave the judgment as to the reasonableness—and therefore the authoritativeness— of a law to the common citizenry, you will have something like anarchy.

The question remains. But my answer to the question "Who decides whether an enactment is reasonable?" is "Everybody." Everybody has a right to make this judgment, whether those in authority, under authority, or a third party observing this. And I don't know any way to get around the necessity of this judgment.

Finally, a couple of remarks on the cultural/ecclesial situation. I was quoted last night as saying that there is in the United States culture an "allergy" to authority based to some degree on traditions of individualism and more recently and somewhat powerfully also on a new sense of relativism, which I think is very widespread. Underlying it often is the assumption that authority or power (and it is interesting that those two are often equated, so that Dr. Selznick's careful distinction between power and authority often goes quite unobserved in people's "allergic reaction") is antithetical to freedom.

I think there is a widespread neglect of the degree to which our own individual selves, our persons, our personalities, are—in many respects that have never become fully conscious to ourselves—framed and oriented by various communities, traditions, and authorities.

With regard to the church situation, there is the question of the degree to which many Catholics are in a position to make intelligent judgments on many of the issues that are often controverted. I think that now people taking polls often do differentiate between Catholics who are regularly practicing their faith and those who barely or never enter the church door. I find there is less interest in trying to work out relationships between levels of education or simple knowledge of elementary aspects of the faith and the tradition, on the one hand, and their responses to particular cases, on the other. I think that's a major question.

Finally, there is the question of the degree to which in our church the Pauline criterion that the bishop be an apt teacher, meaning both knowing what to teach and how to teach, in fact enters into the criteria for the selection of men to the episcopate.

JAMES CORIDEN: Let me try to hem you in from the left. I have but three complaints, Joseph, about your paper and they're all three failures to press hard enough. The one is where you talk about the consultative process involved in the two pastorals, *The Challenge of Peace* and *Economic Justice for All*, and the willingness on the part of our bishops to learn before they try to teach. And I just wish that you had pressed those two functions as theological and moral imperatives rather than as, what they might be assumed to be, simply strategies or teaching methodologies. I don't think they should be optional.

Second, where you say—and here your subtext blames canon lawyers, and that's why I have to rise to their defense—that teaching authority is looked upon as binding force and that we speak often of obeying church teaching rather than believing in it or assenting to it. It is the attempt to teach by compulsion or the juridicizing of the teaching office. Teaching by decree. Ordering belief. Commanding assent. You didn't hit it hard enough. It is a far worse disease in our heritage than you allege.

Finally, you discuss the dangers of purely formal authority obliging assent simply on the basis of the authority of the office from which the enactment comes. It is enough that the enactment comes from the empowered office. Of course, you're not agreeing with this, but you don't unmask it thoroughly enough. The reliance on formal authority, authority derived only from office without giving reasons for decisions, ought to be condemned.

AVERY DULLES: Basically, I think I agreed with most of the paper, so I found little to complain about. I thought you might say more than you did about the teaching authority of episcopal conferences, but I think we're in substantial agreement there. At least, I'd like to try out on you the idea that they do not really have autonomous teaching authority, and they cannot by themselves establish doctrine to be believed, but rather their function is to apply the doctrine of the universal church to the local situation in the region where they are established. So, we're not moving from a monocentric to a polycentric church in which there would be kind of autonomous regional churches, but really we do have a Roman center of authority with, not branch offices, but nevertheless local churches that are in communion with Rome as the center of communion.

And in one of my articles, which I think you referred to in a footnote, I speak of conferences having a pastoral rather than a strictly doctrinal magisterium. I'd like to know whether you think that's a suitable expression. That is just a question.

On the question of whether authority should give reasons or not, I am inclined to say maybe in many cases it's better not to give reasons. I have read Newman, as Father Komonchak has, and he is very sensitive to the fact that you can have reasons that you cannot articulate and that the tradition really is the bearer of these unarticulated reasons. That's why you need to have tradition in the church, because not everything is spelled out verbally. Rather, it is implicit in the mode of action, the way of worship of the church, and so forth. It can't be explicitated, and when you do try to give reasons, often you raise more questions because reasons call for counter reasons and you immediately think of all the reasons on the other side. So, Montini, I think, had a very fine statement quoted in your footnote: "Le propre de l'autorité, c'est de ne pas se justifier (The distinguishing mark of authority is that it doesn't justify itself)." I think there is a lot to be said for that.

And really, faith is an acceptance of authority, and if we don't accept the authority of the church, we're not Catholics any longer.

JOSEPH KOMONCHAK: Well, I am in an enviable position here. With regard to Jim Coriden's comments, they're not really criticisms but suggestions that I should have been more forceful. I certainly do think that nobody, whether a bishop or anybody else, should try to teach before he has learned.

I certainly do think, however the process is undertaken, that it is simply necessary, if a bishop or a conference of bishops or, for that matter the pope, has a new question arising, that they don't try to solve it simply by going to their chapel and praying fervently. They also have to think. And if they are not in a position to do the kind of work that is necessary, then they have to get other people to do that kind of work and then to make some sort of judgment about it. So, I agree with Jim on that.

I also think that the juridicizing of the teaching and the equating of teaching in the church with passing laws has been very, very harmful—has had very, very harmful effects upon theology and practices of the magisterium in the church. I've written a good deal about that elsewhere. I was moving rapidly in this article.

With regard to Father Dulles's comment about the teaching authority of episcopal conferences, I think that we would both agree, Avery and I, over and against the position that in effect denied that episcopal conferences have any teaching authority. I think that we would agree that they do have some teaching authority. I don't think that I would express it quite in the way that Avery just did.

It's true that they can't establish doctrine for the universal church. They do not represent a supreme exercise of the church's teaching authority. That certainly is true. That their only function is the application of the teaching of the universal church, I'm not as convinced. For me, that suggests that there is a sense in which the church is already in the possession at least of the principles from which would come the response to almost any question that might arise, and that, therefore, the sole function of the episcopal conferences would be to consult what the church already teaches and believes and from it to draw the appropriate applications to its own country, particularly in pastoral matters. I think that's far too simplistic.

The sharp disjunction between principles and applications simply doesn't necessarily work hermeneutically or philosophically. But the other issue is the question of what happens when new questions arise, and here, to refer again to our common master, Newman, he regretted the fact that all kinds of intermediate instances of authority which existed and flourished during the Middle Ages for addressing new questions as they arose on a local level, whether among theological faculties, or provincial councils, or whatever, had mostly disappeared. And that now, and perhaps he was thinking of his own case, the theologian found himself naked before the effectively omnipotent Roman authority. There was no intermediate stage.

For me, the question arises when new forms, new questions need to be, and perhaps legitimately can be, addressed on local levels? You don't have to go immediately to the supreme and universal authority to address them. So I would not, to answer your particular question, reduce the teaching authority of episcopal conferences, any more than that of an individual bishop, simply to a question of pastoral authority.

As to the question of whether it is good to give reasons: The quotation from the-then-Msgr. Montini that I cite in my footnote, I drew from a biography of Étienne Gilson, who recalled it when Montini was elected pope. Gilson was still angry and upset at the comment that was made to him when he had gone to Msgr. Montini to defend Father Chenu—his book had been just placed on the Index—and said, "I found only four places in the whole book in which he addresses any doctrinal issues at all. On three of them he is clearly orthodox. The fourth one you might want to say is a little ambiguous but it is certainly not clearly heretical. So, why was this book condemned?" And that's when Montini said, "The distinguishing mark of authority is that it doesn't justify itself."

Well, there is a sense in which, as my description of how authority functions in the university shows, I agree. I mean, when you go in and start teaching a course, you don't set out all your reasons for every assertion or you would never get beyond the first assertion. And in fact, you have lost authority if, every time you mention something—my example was, "in less than 100 days after he was elected, Pope John XXIII startled the Catholic world by announcing he was going to convoke an ecumenical council." Well, there are at least ten dimensions of that. You don't have any authority if a student puts his hand up immediately and says, "Prove it!" In effect, your ability to teach without giving reasons, or all of the reasons every single time, is an indication of your authority. So, there is that truth in it.

For me, the more important question is whether, in order to teach, you need to have reasons. On controverted issues, I would say you need to have them. Now, your main reason may be saying, "Listen, we have behind this a long, long tradition and traditions are not, should not be, lightly overthrown." Now, that in itself could be a reason, and I think you could make that case. But I think you need to have reasons. I don't think you would want to make a decision on a genuinely disputed question in the church on which, to all external appearances, sincere and intelligent and good Christians disagree, without giving reasons. You have to have some reasons for your decision, it seems to me. If challenged on it, in the normal case you should be required to, you should want to, set out the reasons that led to the decision. So, I'd be inclined to say that if there are any circumstances in which it is not a good thing to give reasons, I hope that they are very, very few.

JAMES CORIDEN

JAMES CORIDEN: Let me begin by saying how happy I am to be among you. I'd just like to remind you of four points that I made briefly in the paper which I do think are terribly important in any consideration of this kind. The first one is the issue of Christian freedom, which perhaps is being assumed by everybody talking about authority, but I don't think it should be assumed.

I think the freedom of Christians—of Catholics even within their own church—is a very basic concept and should not be passed over. I touch on it very briefly among the introductory remarks.

Second, I talk about authority in the New Testament and how authority is described there. The authority that is passed down to the church is described, particularly as articulated by Jesus, as service. That seems to me a central teaching, not a peripheral teaching, in all four gospels, and it is associated with the very mission and ministry of Christ himself. That is a starting place and a touchstone for the whole concept of authority that we cannot gainsay nor depart from.

Third, that sacred power, the power of governance in the church, is not a matter just for the ordained; it is quite clearly a thing in which all of the faithful participate. I touched on it very briefly, but again, I think it is one of the radical points of departure for conciliar teaching, that the first place of infallibility is the church, not the magisterium *within* the church, *the church*. The first authority is that of all of the faithful or of all of those within whom the Spirit dwells. And then certain people have offices within that community of disciples. But it is, first of all, the authority of the church.

And finally, the principle of subsidiary function, which is very important to the problem of authority within the church and the way it is exercised. Authority within the church has been overly centralized.

But the heart of my paper is the cases. That's why I labeled it *Cases and Observations*. I really meant the cases to be the fodder for our discussion, because cases unearth all sorts of things—people's reactions to concrete decisions, real situations where there are real options. What did they do? What could they have done? What should they have done?

The first case, the general absolution case, is really meant to point to the ability and the need for pastoral accommodation. As Paul VI and the synod of 1967 put it, a *congrua potestas discretionis*—an appropriate power of discretion on the part of the faithful and on the part of the pastors. An appropriate room within which to live, to move. An appropriate response to any norm, particularly disciplinary norms, is not lockstep, not the same the world round, not precisely the same in this socioeconomic situation as in that. There must be appropriate room for discretionary action.

We've lost sight of that kind of pastoral accommodation, it seems to me. Cardinal Bernardin seems to epitomize it in the case.

The second case is about what is sometimes called the internal-forum solution to the divorced and remarried. Again, moral discernment is the more important factor here than subsidiary function, which also comes into play. We have over-juridicized the pastoral situation of divorced and remarried Catholics. We have reduced it to a juridical determination of the status of persons (taking over a Roman law process for determining who is a Roman citizen and who is not). We apply it to the question of who is married and who isn't, and address that pastoral situation in that extremely narrow way, and I think in a way that can no longer be tolerated.

A more appropriate response to that human reality of the divorced and remarried is imperative at this point, for our church. And that's why the canon lawyers don't invite me places anymore either!

Finally, the last case is on conflict resolution, and that's simply the American belief in due process. If you have effective grievance procedures in place and believe in them and use them, you save yourself an infinite amount of grief, and you give a great deal of satisfaction to those who feel that they have been heard. And I don't understand why we don't make more use of what are commonplace kinds of grievance procedures.

JOSEPH KOMONCHAK: I noticed no self-criticism, however.

JAMES CORIDEN: My self-criticism is that I am overly optimistic about human nature.

JOSEPH KOMONCHAK: Just a couple of remarks. First of all, it's clear from the beginning and the end of the paper that Jim wants to make a very clear distinction—a major distinction—between the nature, grounds, and exercise of authority in the church and elsewhere. And the question I'm raising is, To what degree is church authority *sui generis* (unique unto itself) and how does the purpose of authority, which, of course, he rightly sets out in his paper, cash out in its exercise?

At times, I had a little bit of a feeling that you thought it was enough to invoke words like *freedom* and *salvation* as if that ended the issue. It seems to me there are very complex issues there.

Second, on Vatican II, you suggest that Vatican II is rather clear on the laity's participation in all three functions of the teaching, governing, and saving. I wonder whether you're not perhaps exaggerating the degree to which the council was willing to grant to laypeople a real role in the governance authority. It seems to me that when you start looking through *Lumen gentium,* you find it's much clearer on teaching, much clearer on saving—on the participation there—than it is on governance. As a matter of fact, I think Hans Küng wrote a long article criticizing *Lumen gentium* on that ground.

So, there is a genuine debate among the canonists and the theologians today on the relationship between the power of orders and the power of governance. You clearly are coming down on the side that the power or governing function should be, or can legitimately be, differentiated from the question of ordination. It seems to me the whole move of the council was in fact trying to reintegrate those two aspects of the office of the bishop.

Finally, the question of the relevance of subsidiarity within the church. As a general principle, I find it unexceptionable. Your position I would agree with, and I wrote a long article to argue the case. I do think, also, that it needs to be applied so that much more freedom and authority are acknowledged to reside in individual churches and in regional groups. But I think also we have to recognize that the principle remains a purely formal principle, in effect saying as much freedom as possible and as much order or intervention or whatever is necessary, and that it can't serve by itself to settle controverted issues. It can't serve as a kind of magic wand. And I find that that at times is a problem in some of these discussions.

Trying to settle, for example, when is an intervention of higher authority legitimate in a particular case? Is it in fact the case that the local authority, which ought to have been able to handle a question, did not in fact handle it well, and it was for the good of the church that a higher authority intervened? Those often involve you in very concrete questions. I often find the answers to them being settled on a priori ideological or theological grounds, so that when it was my friend who got interfered with it was bad and a violation of the principle of subsidiarity, and when it was some person I don't like who got removed, I say, "Oh, good, that's why we have a pope."

AVERY DULLES: I think I have a lot to agree with and yes, Christian freedom of course is wonderful, provided it is really Christian. I think we have to keep in mind that Jesus said the truth shall make you free and that Paul speaks of the freedom with which Christ has made us free. It does not mean simply self-determination. And authority of service is fine. Of course, everybody agrees to that, but that does not mean that the people who are served necessarily dictate to the servants, because it can be authoritative service with a genuine power of obligation.

Regarding due-process procedures, I think I agree entirely with what you say so far as I was able to assimilate it. On the other two questions that you discuss, the questions of general absolution and the internal-forum—improperly so-called—solutions on marriage cases, I do think that there is a doctrinal issue involved in each of those and that Rome does have a legitimate concern to protect the integrity of the sacraments. Thus they had a reason to say that normally the sacrament of penance has a kind of judicial and medicinal aspect to it that is better implemented where it is administered individually rather than collectively in some kind of collective absolution, so that the penance is proportionate to the sin and the sinner has explicitly confessed, and so forth. So, I don't think general absolution should be too readily adopted.

With the divorced and remarried, I think Rome was concerned, and is legitimately concerned, not to make this infringe on the indissolubility of marriage and in effect to validate divorce and remarriage in the church.

Although I am convinced that there are serious doctrinal issues involved here, I'm not saying what the ultimate solution ought to be. I know there has been a very interesting discussion between the German bishops and Rome on this point in the last few years, which you didn't allude to but I'm sure you had in mind, and I'm not making any judgment on how that should come out. But I think there are doctrinal issues. It is not simply a disciplinary question that can be solved locally.

JAMES CORIDEN: I don't really have much to say in response to those remarks, all of which I agree with. There are similarities between the way authority is exercised within and without the church. I was trying to point out the dissimilarities.

The foundation within the council documents of the participation of the laity in the disciplinary authority, ruling or pastoring authority, is certainly not as clear as the laity's share in the teaching authority, but the foundation, the theological foundation, is there. I think you're quite right: they were trying to unite the sacramental and juridical authority rather than separate them as they had been, unfortunately. But I think that the doctrinal foundation is there, and I think it needs to be built upon.

And I think that the canonical debate on lay governance is moving in that direction. I think that that debate is nearing an end.

I have much less a problem with self-determination, Avery, than you do. You remark in your paper that people did what they thought was right because the debate was not resolved; I think that is the appropriate course of action rather than an aberration. And that's why I like the theme of freedom to be often sounded. I find that it is not. And that can lead us astray. Hence, my remark about being overly optimistic about human nature. One has to remember what Thomas Aquinas used to repeat on occasion: "Infinitus est numerus stultorum," that there are many stupid people and many of us are in need of direction and guidance.

There are doctrinal issues involved in both the second-marriage question and in general absolution, but in both we are desperately in need of a better pastoral approach than we have now. And simply to say that there are doctrinal issues involved, as you put it quite accurately, does not predetermine the pastoral outcome. The recent discussion between the bishops of the Upper Rhine and Cardinal Ratzinger is a very good case in point. Unresolved.

In Summation

Robert Imbelli: Thank you all very much. I think that really did what we were hoping would be done. So, we appreciate that.

I had reserved to myself the possibility of raising some questions, which thankfully I did not have to do, but I would like to raise three issues that are in my mind, and in perhaps some of your minds, that I would like to hear about more from the panelists.

As I read Avery Dulles's paper, he makes reference to the *sensus fidelium,* and yet I read it as a very wary reference. And so, if I am right in that, if my Italian intuition is working, I'd like to hear a little more about that from Avery. Why the wariness, if indeed there is wariness? And I'd also like some help in trying to come to grips with it. I think there is almost a promiscuous appeal today to *sensus fidelium,* and I think it would be a contribution if we did get some further clarity on the issue.

With regard to Joseph Komonchak's paper, he has a quotation from Bernard Lonergan, in which there's an evocation of conversion and the importance of conversion (see chapter 2, note 15, above). Now, I know Joe well enough to know that that's not put in as sort of a pious little footnote. I think it is much more germane to his analysis, and I'd like to ask how so.

I mean, it is only tangentially touched upon. I think some of those considerations of the importance of conversion have a bearing, both on officeholders and upon those who receive the teaching.

My final point is with regard to Jim Coriden's paper, and this both gives me an opportunity to refer to Professor Selznick's paper and to bring him into the discussion. One of the things I derived from Selznick's paper was his insistence on the need for an objective order based on shared values, principles, and institutions—that this was not just a *desideratum* but a real need.

Now, I read the final portion of his paper (the section "Authority in the Church") as in some sense sketching such an objective order with regard to church authority. But a question I would raise to Jim, despite his last quote from Thomas Aquinas, is, Does he worry about the viability of such an objective order in a culture in which authority, according to Selznick, becomes "inherently instable and placative"? Does that worry Jim, the possibility of maintaining the desired objective order within such a culture?

As Avery responded, we would all agree on the centrality of service in any Christian understanding of authority—but what do you do in a culture where service is construed in a therapeutic mode? So, we have service industries.

Those are the types of questions that I, for one, have, and perhaps they reflect some of your own concerns. And now, it is a great pleasure to present Professor Philip Selznick.

PHILIP SELZNICK

Thank you very much. I'll just say a word or two about this general discussion and then add a couple of points as an addendum to what I wrote in my paper, things I should have included but did not.

One theme that pervades much of this discussion is the distinction between formal authority or ultimate authority and the ways that authority is exercised. We have this problem in many contexts, and certainly in religious contexts. Granting that there is, let's say, ultimate authority in God or in the Bible or what have you, how is that authority to be interpreted? And how is it to be exercised?

The more we look at the difference between formal authority and effective authority, or between the locus of authority and the practice of authority, the more likely we are to see some connection between the two. So the question is whether the way authority is exercised does not raise questions about the need for reconstruction of formal authority.

I don't want to get into issues that are really beyond my competence, but it seems obvious that to speak of authority in God does not settle the question of how that authority should be understood. It does not tell us where God's authority resides, so far as human institutions are concerned.

Let me say a few words about some other matters. In my paper I was writing a little bit about the ambient American culture and I think I said that distrust of authority is a lively passion and a beguiling heritage. Beguiling because it may lead people to misjudge the significance of mistrusting authority and the cost of that distrust. Within our political world, for example, distrust of authority may severely limit what we as a community can do together, the kinds of collective judgments we can make, the kinds of institutions that we can create for dealing with our common problems.

What I did *not* say, was that any discussion of culture ought to include principles of evaluation. There's always that tension. On the one hand, we think that when a culture has developed, we ought to respect it, and we do so in many ways. On the other hand, no culture is entitled to absolute respect. We may want to say that the culture is too thin to sustain the important disciplines of everyday life, of child rearing, for example, and so on. We may want to say of the culture that it is impoverished in various ways, perhaps even that it is demonic, but perhaps more generally that it is simply incapable of, or provides roadblocks to, the exercise of practical reason through collective institutions.

So, the worth of cultures is not absolute, and everyone has to make judgments. Every institution has to make judgments about what aspects of American culture, for example, ought to be taken seriously as positive contributions to our common well-being and what aspects of American culture ought to be resisted and criticized.

Which brings me to another point I didn't mention in my paper, which bears on the relation between American history and American culture. What I have in mind is the problem of inclusion. We have seen enormous changes not only in the relation between sex and marriage and similar matters but also in our awareness of deprivations suffered by women and minorities, in our sense of responsibility for future generations, in connection with environmental issues. These are positive changes in American culture. We could go into the reasons why they are positive, but the relevant point here is that they raise questions of inclusion in the exercise of church authority, not only in the relation between clergy and laity but also the very structure of authority within the church. Who participates? Who is taken seriously? Who is marginalized? All these, I think, are major issues.

I'd also like to say something about another aspect of culture. I suppose it's one of the fairly important contributions of modern social science that we have come to a much better understanding of the role of culture in large organizations. We have come to understand how easy it is for the history of an organization to create a culture that may advance or undermine its fundamental purposes or values.

Someone asked me last night to say what one meant by culture. A group has a culture insofar as it manifests patterned ways of thinking, feeling, communicating, and valuing. These patterns can be found within particular institutions as well as in the society as a whole.

The organizational culture of the Catholic Church includes a remarkably rich institutional texture, upheld and to a large extent embodied in a church hierarchy. What I do not see in these discussions are the reasons to justify the hierarchy. I do not doubt that those reasons can be given, but I do think that if we make them clear and explicit it will be easier to diagnose the institution's difficulties. What virtues are to be enhanced? In what ways? What dangers arise from arrogant or prideful exercise of authority? How are they to be mitigated? In other words, what is taken for granted by everybody is that the hierarchy or magisterium is basically a good thing. Not so clear are the reasons that make it good. The issue is diagnosis, not justification.

This concern for reasons, given and not given, reminds me of a passage in Winston Churchill's history of the Second World War. One unlucky bomb had demolished the chamber of the House of Commons. The problem arose as to the rebuilding of the chamber and the principles that should govern that rebuilding. The two basic principles, Churchill said, are not well understood. Tradition calls for a chamber that is rectangular rather than semicircular and that is too small to hold all of the members at one time. Churchill said that many new members find this puzzling indeed. But he offered some reasons. The chamber should be small enough to encourage a conversational style in ordinary meetings—and this is the part I like the best— in a small chamber there will be on great occasions a sense of crowd and urgency.

Well, here was Churchill, the historian, writing about parliamentary architecture, reflecting on reasons not articulated. New members and, for that matter, the British public simply accept the tradition. But there are reasons, and they are important. If you explicate the reasons, you better understand the practical and perhaps modify it in ways that preserve fundamental values.

Finally, I would like to say a word about what I think is central to our concerns—the idea of responsiveness. In most institutions, to enhance the acceptance of authority we say the institution should be more responsive. Responsiveness is a very tricky idea. You can be a responsive administrator in a university, for example, or think you are, if you yield to all pressures. But that's opportunism, not responsiveness.

A responsive institution tries to balance a full commitment to basic purposes and, at the same time, be aware of, take account of, new circumstances, new interests, valid claims. So, to be responsive is to exercise judgment. There is no escape from judgment. We have to judge the validity of claims. No principle of institutional design will free us from that responsibility.

Note

[1] Father Komonchak is referring to a paper distributed as background for the participants—Joseph Komonchak, "Authority and Magisterium," in *Vatican Authority and American Catholic Dissent,* ed. William W. May (New York: Crossroad, 1987), 103–14.

6

FIRST GENERAL DISCUSSION

JOHN NOONAN: I'd like to comment on Avery's paper because I think nobody could disagree with the theory as expounded, but if you believed that God had come to earth and set out a program for the rest of life on this earth, you would think the way Avery spoke. But then you might read some history.

Now, Avery, you did say the exercise of authority may lead to some mistakes. The record is replete with mistakes. And you've got to take that into account when you say, "What does the assistance of God to Peter and his successors mean?" If you look at the historical record, you see that the assistance of God does not mean that they will not make a number of fairly gross mistakes. The teaching on religious liberty may stand for all of them.

Therefore, the faithful can't just accept everything that comes from Rome as though God had authorized it. You have to be aware there may be a big mistake, and you have to have some provision for that dissent to be acted upon and to finally persuade the authorities to revise the doctrine as they did after about fifteen hundred years in the case of religious liberty, only thirty-five years ago.

AVERY DULLES: I think there should be some provision for revision of doctrine, and not all doctrinal statements are infallible.

But I would have to study the question of the history of this religious freedom somewhat to see just where the doctrinal errors were. Could you point out a particular doctrinal error on this?

JOHN NOONAN: Yes. Up until 1964, if people were in heresy, it was proper to coerce them, or coerce them psychologically anyway, and if it was a Catholic state you could coerce them by physical force. That was the standard teaching. You can see it in the works of Cardinal Ottaviani or any of the continental moralists up till the council. John Courtney Murray was a lonely voice to the contrary, and he was silenced when he expressed his totally dissenting view. Then the council wonderfully transformed it. While the ordinary magisterium, all the bishops, all the theologians had taught that the repression of heresy was the proper thing for any Catholic state, the council goes to almost the other extreme in saying even psychological coercion is contrary to revelation and to reason. It's about as 180–degree shift as one has ever seen.

You've got to grapple with that fact, Avery, or you just don't understand what has happened in the history of our church.

AVERY DULLES: Well, I think there is a very long tradition in favor of freedom of conscience and the freedom of the act of faith. And I'm not aware that any papal statement ever contradicted that. I don't think that John Courtney Murray was condemned for teaching that conscience should not be coerced.

I think the issues were quite different. They had to do with the establishment of religion in the state. Murray himself always taught that there was nothing against the establishment of a religion in a state, although he also said that it is possible to have an order in which no religion is established. You could have a secular state in which a variety of religions were equally tolerated. But that, I think, is a different issue from the coercion of conscience.

JOHN NOONAN: Well, I think you misstate the issues. It is not the coercion of conscience. It is the coercion of heretics. That was the doctrine.

AVERY DULLES: Yes, well—

JOHN NOONAN: A person who was a baptized Christian, who departed from the faith, then the freedom of the act of faith was not at stake. The question was, Could that person be coerced into accepting orthodox faith? And that was a teaching of St. Augustine and numerous popes and all theologians up until 1964.

AVERY DULLES: Well, if so, I think it contradicted other elements in the Catholic tradition, and I don't think Murray saw himself as dissenting but simply as carrying on the most Christian and valid elements in the Catholic tradition. And I don't think he ever considered himself a dissenter.

JOSEPH KOMONCHAK: I don't think we want to get into the details of that particular question.

BENEDICT ASHLEY: It was a wonderful discussion. The thing I got out of it though, in a practical sense, was that our problem is certainly that of persuasion. I believe authority ought to be obeyed, even when they don't give good reasons. But it certainly works better when they can—when what they say is plausible. And I think that the present pope makes a tremendous effort to explain why he has taken the positions that he has taken.

However, his reasons don't get heard. It's partly his own style, but I think it's inevitable that somebody in his position speaking to the whole world is going to have a very hard time being very persuasive, particularly when he runs up against some issue like the one of women's ordination or contraception. It is very hard to be persuasive about those issues. It doesn't mean, however, that they're not true.

Consequently, it seems to me that perhaps the direction of Common Ground ought to be primarily to get a real hearing for the magisterial positions. I must say that I don't think in this country that most of our leading theologians make much of an effort to explain to the public or to the press the reasonableness of these positions. They're usually almost automatically attacked. That's why I think that the strategy, if we can call it that, in the church at the present moment, which is really the direction the bishops seem to be going, is to put the emphasis on the notion of the *Catechism of the Catholic Church*.

The *Catechism* may be defective, but it is a solid statement of the heritage of the church. If it were widely understood that that is the heritage of the church, many of these magisterial positions would become more credible and even the criticisms of them would become more really intelligible. It seems to me that we ought to favor that. Now let me say one more thing.

I'm worried about Common Ground because last time I suggested that more people having a clearly conservative stamp on them who would be heard by conservatives would be represented in the group. There are not many. I have asked about this. I understand it is because the conservatives won't come. Now, I think it is the duty of the bishops to say to people on both sides of the spectrum, for the good of the church, you have to be in this dialogue.

GERRY SHEA: I would add my thanks for a wonderfully thoughtful and collegial panel discussion. I thought it all moved together very well and was helpful.

But I found myself wanting to hear more about what you might say about the greater church, the receiving end of decision-making. You talked some about the interaction between those in authority and those below authority but I just wondered if you would care to say anything more about what you think are the important characteristics or important dynamics that are going on among the people in the church as to this gap that we've been talking about?

JOSEPH KOMONCHAK: That's an awfully big question, but I'll try to set out a few of my ecclesiological presuppositions since that was the kind of a question that Jim Coriden raised and to some degree it moves in on this issue. I think that the basic mystery of the church's life and its realization occur on the local level, beginning with small communities of faith. To that degree it is the exact opposite of a phrase, an unfortunate phrase that I think Avery used—although having read him for many, many years, I don't think it would encapsulate his approach to the church—when he referred to the universal church and then to branch offices.

AVERY DULLES: I said I didn't hold to branch offices.

JOSEPH KOMONCHAK: But it was in a context where it suggested that there was something of that sort going on. In any case, I think it is a mistake to approach the fundamental issue of whether there is a church or whether there should be a church or what the state of the church is from a universalistic standpoint.

The fundamental question of whether there is a church is something that is settled in this place and that place, at this time and at that time, and it is settled by the fundamental communication of the mystery of Jesus Christ and whether that is communicated or not. It's 1 John 1:1–4: "What we have seen and heard we communicate to you, we announce to you so that you may have communion with us and our communion is with the Father and with his Son, Jesus Christ, and we are writing to you so that our joy may be complete—full." That is the fundamental level at which it seems to me there is a church or there is not a church.

Now, that is not contradictory to the notion that there is one church because the one church is the communion of all of those churches, but it makes a big difference whether the first thing that comes into your mind is the universal organization or the local experience.

So, the issue that you are raising is—and for me this is crucial—what is the vitality of faith on the local level? And it's at that level that I have some major fears. I'm responding to your question about how well we are communicating what we saw and heard to a new generation. To what degree are we communicating the joy of our own communion, which will not be complete unless a new generation is brought into that? And that ties in with my other question. I think that these other issues that have been raised here are unintelligible outside a genuine prior communion in that fundamental mystery. And they can be rendered intelligible or reasonable in a Christian theological sense only from within that center. If that is not secure, we could spend from now until doomsday talking about contraception or the ordination of women or whatever and not come to any kind of resolution. That's the common ground that I would like to be assured is present.

My general fear—I don't have empirical evidence for this apart from the profound ignorance that is characteristic of our incoming students into the Catholic University of America—is that central elements of the faith simply are not part of their knowledge or even experience. And if you don't secure the center, if you don't communicate that well, it seems to me it is impossible to resolve these issues.

CYPRIAN DAVIS: I had mentioned to Father Coriden that I appreciated very much the use of the case method and I think it's very good. I would go much further, however, and say that we should really put each instance into a historical context, because when we look at many of these questions and talk about historical development, some things would cause us to pause or to nuance a little differently.

For example, in 1849 Pope Gregory XVI wrote an apostolic brief in which he condemned the slave trade. He condemned it in very harsh language. He also forbade any Christian, any Catholic Christian, lay or ecclesiastic, to defend it publicly. Personally, I think it was a good idea. And many would say by implication he condemned slavery itself.

John England was the bishop of Charleston, and here you have a clear case of subsidiarity. He began, first of all, by saying that Gregory XVI was no abolitionist, which, of course, was a defense supposedly of the pope, since being an abolitionist was a dirty word. He also went about trying to prove that the church had never condemned slavery. In fact, he said the church had always supported it and Gregory XVI was talking about what those Portuguese and those Spanish were doing, not what was being done here in the United States—that's not trafficking in slaves.

So, I think one of the things you have to look at in terms of authority and the development of authority, even through the centuries in the church, is that often enough the papal authority increased not because it did it itself, but because on the local level they found a relief from local subsidiarity, which is often tyrannical. The Pseudo-Isidorian Decretals is a famous example of this. Another example is Benedict XV, in *Maximum illud,* where he says that there should be a native clergy encouraged. There should be a native hierarchy. On the local level, the bishops who were all French in China, for example, didn't want Chinese bishops. It was the intervention of a higher authority on the side of the native people, of the people of the area.

JOSEPH KOMONCHAK: I'm very glad you brought up the cases there. For me, it illustrates the fact that you cannot place complete trust in any particular level of authority. The example of Benedict XV is a good one. He was the one who promoted the indigenization of the clergy in Africa as well, and he was resisted by most of the local bishops. And if there had not been that kind of an intervention on the part of Benedict XV, followed up in practice by several of his successors, then there would never have been that move. And I think it's a very good example.

On the level of theory, it means in effect that there is a necessity of discernment and of judgment at all of these levels. And if you go back historically and try to make some kind of judgment, you're going to find at times that the authentic evangelical call came from the highest levels and at other times it came from the lowest levels. And there would be times that, at the highest levels in fact, the evangelical call was either ignored or denied or sometimes downright contradicted. I don't think there is any objective criterion out there that excuses either the pope vis-à-vis the bishops, the bishops vis-à-vis the pope, the faithful vis-à-vis pope and bishops, from their own responsibilities to take the Gospel seriously, to exercise their own intelligence and responsibility for being faithful to the Gospel.

ANNE E. PATRICK: The issue of tyranny that Cyprian Davis brought up in terms of the local bishop, and the issue of faith that Joe Komonchak has been speaking of, both connect to something that I brought to our table. This is my question: In pressing the sacred/secular dichotomy, are we exempting official church structures from the political analysis that allows us to use this word *tyranny,* for example, as Cardinal Newman used it? And I sense implicit in the writings of Archbishop John Quinn, and the article by Bishop Matthew Clark,[1] which we were given to study, that they had experienced something like tyranny in Newman's sense.

And while this discussion is going on at one level, there is the pragmatic pastoral issue of elitism in view of the desire of many Catholics for a simple premodern way of relating to God, to the sacred, without critical thought. So the attitude is, "I believe because it is absurd, I am exercising the muscle of faith against all reason. Don't give me reasons. Don't complicate my life. Let it be simple. Let me place my absolute faith in this authority."

It makes life simpler for those exercising authority when there is that kind of docility operative, but it's very problematic for the educated elites. And I don't think that the issue of where the sacred is and how much critical reason must be removed from the sacred, from our experience of sacrality, and from our worship of God, has been addressed sufficiently. I believe that is a latent issue here.

SCOTT APPLEBY: Following up on Anne's comment, I thought what Joe Komonchak said a few moments ago was one of the most important statements made yet about the presupposition of communion in this room that is not shared by so many of the people that we are concerned about in Common Ground. And in this regard, the conversation here is almost as if we would be speaking into a void.

In the culture today, one of the things that I think happens among Catholic students and older Catholics as well, is the operative assumption of what was condemned in 1907 as "vital immanence," that is, an in-dwelling presence and an immediate contact with the divine that is not mediated by the tradition or by church authority. The operative assumption of many students, and also older Catholics, is that the category of experience is primary and that any kind of appeal to authority has to connect to their "experience," whatever that term might mean. Consequently, when we begin to address a question like should we give reasons for our teaching, that question seems irrelevant to the culture we face. Of course, there have to be reasons. Furthermore, there have to be reasons that have some direct contact with the experience of the people who are being addressed and how they understand experience. And that's why I come back to the condemnation of vital immanence. The assumption that has to be challenged in the culture is this: If I have a twinkle or a twinge in my toes and a feeling of spirituality and a closeness to my fellow Christian or fellow student, that is sufficient to enter into this kind of communion.

So in summary I want to say there are some basic assumptions culturally that we haven't yet fully addressed that need to be addressed when we talk about authority.

BRIAN DALEY: I wanted just to underline what seems to me very important in a number of the comments that were made this morning, and also in Joe Komonchak's paper, and that is the distinction between the authority of teaching and what we might call juridical authority, the authority of executives, and so on. It really is a very different notion of authority, and it has different criteria for its credibility and its reception.

It seems to me that in the church all authority comes down not simply to teaching authority, but at least to preaching authority. The institutions that we have, the structures that come from apostolic times, are structures which are there in order to safeguard and to communicate the Gospel, the message about Jesus and about his teaching, and the effects on us of his resurrection, and so on.

Certainly, in the early church, beginning with the pastoral letters, the understanding of authority in the church is always seen as growing out of the necessity of preaching the Gospel in an authentic way. And preaching has a whole different set of criteria for its authenticity, I think, than does the authority of an executive in a corporation or even of a teacher in a classroom. I am not saying that preaching is necessarily always monologic, or that it doesn't give reasons for what it says. Surely theology, the explanation of the message, is central, too, to the life of the church. But ultimately, I think, the authority of the preacher comes from the message. And the message itself is understood, in some way, to be proclaimed as something set before the hearers. There is a prophetic character, I think, to authority in the church which really is the reason for the freedom that Avery is talking about, the freedom to take unpopular decisions in a final way, and for some of the other characteristics people have been pointing out here. I think it is something that we haven't averted to enough in our theological reflections on authority in the church. Its root is in preaching and proclamation.

MICHAEL NOVAK: There are more Catholics in Eastern Europe than there are in the United States. In the last fifty years they went through a terrifying experience—beatings, imprisonments, killings—that bears on what we're talking about. Because there was the pope, and because there was communion with Rome, very few bishops, I think none, betrayed the faith. Unlike any other institution in Eastern Europe, the church stood firm. In large part this was because it was not in the power of bishops to capitulate on their own. They were in communion with the church universal, over which they had no power to decide. They were able to say, "I can't do what you ask. That's not in my authority." That was the tremendous service the papacy provided to the church in Eastern Europe—it was the rock on which the bishops stood. We shouldn't forget that. We belong to a faith that is much bigger than any of us. Its visible symbol is the pope.

Second, our community, more than any religious community in the world, gives reasons. We believe in giving reasons. That's what the new *Catechism* is for. Whitehead pointed out that without that tutoring, modern science would not be possible, that is, without the habit of giving reasons for everything. Even to the extent of building universities, promoting inquiry, and so forth. We believe in giving reasons.

The third point, dissenters are often wrong. I just want to say that because people suggest that dissenters are often right. Yes, sometimes dissenters are right, but the probabilities of that are rather low. If you look at history, there are a lot more pretended prophets than there are real prophets. In my lifetime I've seen a lot of dissent fade and disappear. Including some of my own.

Finally, on religious liberty, I know Joe Komonchak rightly didn't want to get into this, but I do think John Noonan oversimplified. For example, the differentiation between economics and politics happened in very recent times, only in the last two hundred years. Before that, the differentiation between religion and politics took a very long time. Frederick II instituted the first laws against heresy in medieval Europe, and he did it—he was no great religious figure—as a crime against the state. His code of law described heresy as more serious than any other crime except treason and the counterfeiting of money.

(Frederick II of Italy was the one who burned down the monastery in which the young Thomas Aquinas was attending school.) In other words, in times past *political* leaders saw the need for consensus in belief, and that view was widespread. It took a long time to emerge out of that. Current notions of religious liberty could not arise until a long evolution in other notions had been achieved.

CATHLEEN KAVENY: I'd like to agree with what Benedict Ashley said about the need to educate people in the basics of Catholicism and the attitudes and the sensibilities and the openness to the mystery that the church bears.

You know, we're all professional Catholics in one way or another in this room. We spend a lot of time thinking and doing and worrying about these sorts of things. Most people go to church on Sunday; they send their kids to CCD from 3:00 to 4:00 on Wednesday afternoon. And that constitutes their training in the church and the framework that they get. So, I don't think these people are likely to be able to appreciate the subtle differences between whether each and every act of marriage has to be open to both goods, or whether the whole marriage has to be open to both goods, in order to accord with what Christ expects.

The problem is that we are missing the institution that can do this. And I go back and I analogize to the legal system, which is where I learned to submit to authority—it was being trained as a lawyer, not being trained in the Catholic Church. As a beginning lawyer trying to be a good lawyer, there were several distinct centers of activity to consider within the whole framework of the legal system. You had the people. You had the scholars at Harvard and Yale and other places advocating the incredible, prophetic, or revolutionary ideas. But you also had the judges doing the "ordinary" work of law, carrying forward in their written opinions the ideas that would shape the ongoing institutional life of the legal community on a day-to-day basis.

And then I tried to analogize those components to the church's situation. Clearly, we've got the theologians, we've got the scholars, advocating the cutting-edge ideas. What we're missing is the analogy to the ongoing opinion writers who, when they write opinions beginning with the word *we,* speak not for themselves but for the institutional context. I think that that really is analogous to preaching, as it should be in the context of the church. But very few homilies convey the ongoing vitality of the church's teachings in a rich way. And maybe the first thing that we need is to reinvigorate preaching so that it will build up the tradition in a way that will allow people to appreciate its riches before we turn to particular neuralgic issues dividing us.

MONIKA HELLWIG: I wanted to underscore a point that was implicit in Komonchak's paper. It has been raised a couple of times and we haven't pursued it. It is the point that we are all called to share the prophetic ministry of Jesus, and that prophecy by its nature is in a certain tension with established authority. The role of established authority is to maintain the status quo, keep things predictable and therefore functioning smoothly, whereas the role of prophecy is to see those matters that are not being attended to.

The best examples in our modern church have been concerned with social justice issues. To maintain the status quo is a task that tends to overlook who is being missed out by the status quo, who is not being included. I think this is more than a social dynamic. It is the Christian vocation to prophesy. To pray. To learn the tradition. To discern and to prophesy. And that will involve a dynamic of change which will be a dynamic of tension.

GERALD FOGARTY: I'd like to support what Scott said and also what Mike Novak said. I've been talking about secularism at my table, but I would link it with this notion of experience— meaning my experience being the final judge—and I find this in terms not only of teaching but also in terms of giving RCIA presentations, where people will say "but that's not my experience." The purpose of the RCIA is to lead you into the experience of the church.

The second thing, in regard to what Mike said: I do agree that sometimes we have to look at exactly what was happening in Eastern Europe to see where the faith was alive and kept. I mean, we can get too American in terms of making some of these judgments. And then finally, just picking up what Cathy said, I am very much aware—I preach every Sunday—of the difference between teaching and preaching. Preaching in my set of categories is a faith-to-faith communication. But it also means that I get immediate feedback right after Mass and that whenever I get attacked, I get attacked always from left and right. Otherwise people are totally indifferent.

JAMES HEFT: I would just like to go back to a theme that I think was present in our discussion this morning and in particular made explicit in Joe Komonchak's paper. That is this necessity of giving reasons. In the New Testament it says that we should be prepared to give reasons for the hope that is in us. It seems to me that that hope is something that transcends simple rationality. It has been suggested that being incorporated into the faith community creates certain predispositions to hear certain things.

For example, if we were to say, "What are the reasons or proof for the resurrection?" Can you give me reasons why I should believe that, or in the real presence, or the Trinity? So, if we could start making some distinctions about the kinds of things for which we can give reasons, the kinds of personal dispositions that we have to presuppose for reasons to be persuasive, then I think we'd be making some headway. I think it was Augustine who once said there are certain things you should understand in order to believe and there are other things you will come to understand only if you believe.

Now, on the other hand, if you say, "You don't agree with me because you're not converted," that gets pretty tricky. It may be because I'm converted and you are not that in fact you don't see my point. Or again, it may not. So, there are a lot of complications here, but I do think if we could begin to work through kinds of teachings for which reasons can be given, the different kinds of reasons, what they presuppose and when, then we might be able to make some headway on Common Ground.

ANN LIN: This comes back to a question a lot of people have raised. I think the people in the pews—and particularly the college students that I'm not that far away from and work with now—come to the church because they have an experience of God. That's where it has to begin. It doesn't end there. Hopefully, if you have an experience of God you are in a community that then teaches you about a tradition of other people who have had an experience with God and how that leads them to believe. And hopefully, if you have an experience of God, you are in a community that says: Guess what? It is not just your heart that gets carried away by the singing, but your head and the intellect that you use in all the rest of your classes that get engaged by this God, too.

And hopefully, if you have an experience of God, you are led to an appreciation of the other people currently living who have an experience of God and know God in different ways and who model to you by their lives and by their actions why you should have faith in what they tell you, even if you don't see all the reasons or believe all the reasons. You're still willing to extend to them the respect that says they may know something that you don't, and you're going to go with that for a while even though you're not giving up what you believe yourself.

I would really like to see this conference focus on how we don't quench people's experience of God, as unformed and uneducated and unreasoning as it might be, before they get led to become less unreasoning and less unformed or more formed or whatever. So, how do we build upon the experience that is there, no matter how partial it is? How do we, maybe as leaders in the hierarchy but maybe also as professional Catholics, model for people in a way that we don't model if we just talk. How do we actually model in our lives why we should believe and what belief does for us?

I would also like to see a greater sense of our own humility in admitting that perhaps we don't always know what the Spirit is, or that our understanding of the Spirit may be wrong, or that our own preparation for transmitting the Spirit may not be enough, whether that preparation comes from our own embeddedness in the culture that we were educated and raised in, or whether it comes from our lack of psychological preparation for ministering to people, or whatever.

AVERY DULLES: I'm giving a course on faith and reason this semester. It is a thing I've been interested in for fifty years, I suppose. There are a lot of distinctions there. I think that what Jim Heft had to say about the need for distinctions is very important. Obviously, the kinds of reasons you can give for things vary a great deal according to the subject matter. St. Thomas Aquinas in *Summa Contra Gentiles* says you shouldn't give reasons for believing in the Trinity and Incarnation and so forth, because the reasons you give will be taken as the reasons why you believe it, and you believe it because of authority—the authority of the revealing God.

But nevertheless, if, as Joe Komonchak says, tradition is a kind of a reason, okay. But it is a reason that rests on authority. So, it is not an intrinsic argument from reason, but we could say loads and loads about that.

Note

[1] Matthew Clark, "The Pastoral Exercise of Authority," *New Theology Review* (August 1997), 6–17.

7

SECOND GENERAL DISCUSSION

ROBERT IMBELLI: I'd like to formulate an observation, ask a question, and then invite the paper writers to comment. I'd like to formulate my observation this way. Yesterday Bryan Hehir made the remark that we here are basically in the 40 to 60 range on a scale of 100 (of conservative/liberal in the church) and the 20s to 80s are missing. It sounds a little bit like the enneagram, but in any case . . .

BRYAN HEHIR: It goes back to when I was a quarterback.

ROBERT IMBELLI: One of the things I thought of—and I forget who is 20 and who is 80—is that very often the extremes would be associated with the category of magisterium and the category of *sensus fidelium*. Very often there is almost a unique emphasis on one or the other of the two categories—hierarchy or people.

My second observation is this. It might be helpful to distinguish how the two groups tend to identify the origin of authority and the mediation of authority. I find that the group that feels most comfortable speaking of magisterium often tends to speak of the origin of authority in terms of Christ. The group that tends to speak of *sensus fidelium* likes to speak of the origin of authority in terms of Spirit. They also, therefore, have different primary mediations of authority—the Twelve (the hierarchy) or the whole community.

Now, within that matrix of observations, which I hope reflects some of the discussion that took place both formally and informally, I pose a question to Avery. Whether this is a correct reading of the paper or not, I notice a certain wariness in appeal to *sensus fidelium* in Avery's paper. I don't remember whether or not Jim used the term, but I would suspect that there would not be an equal wariness or at least as much wariness on his part. So, I wonder whether the panelists might speak to the issue of *sensus fidelium* a little bit more.

AVERY DULLES: Well, obviously there is a lot to be said about *sensus fidelium*. One could speak for half an hour or forty-five minutes easily, but I'll try not to.

I would say the traditional concept of *sensus fidelium* presupposes a Christian community, and it was generally thought up in Catholic cultures where everybody was Catholic and religion permeated the whole social life. I think it gets more and more difficult to apply when you get into a highly secularized society where the majority of the members of the church are not in particularly close contact with the sources of faith, with scripture and tradition and even the magisterium and the sacraments, and their opinions are predominantly formed by a secular context and by the popular media from which they even get their news about the church. It is very difficult for the hierarchy to communicate to the people of God because the diocesan papers are not widely read and people get their news from television reports and *The New York Times* or the *Daily News* or whatever.

So, the *sensus fidelium* is very hard to consult. Who are the *fideles*, the faithful? Now it's quite true that if the *fideles* agree with the pastors, you have a wonderful assurance that this is truly Christian. But where they disagree, you simply have a problem, I think. And one has to analyze the reasons for the disagreement as best one can to see what the solution to the problem might be.

JOSEPH KOMONCHAK: Let me preface this by saying to Bob, my good friend, that I don't understand how you went from the 20/80 to the hierarchy and the *sensus fidelium*. That was not my understanding of the metaphor at all. It had far more to do with the conservatives and liberals. It doesn't break down in terms of hierarchy and faithful. It seems to me important not to make the assumption, as I heard it said when the Common Ground Initiative was first announced, that this is meant to be a place for dialogue between the hierarchy and the laity. It was never intended to be that because one of the motivating purposes, as I understand it, is that even among the body of bishops there was often difficulty in communicating and in acknowledging common ground.

One of the translations of *Lumen gentium* where the phrase *sensus fidelium* appears translates it as a kind of a supernatural instinct of faith. I'm not crazy about the translation, but it points in the direction of what I think may underlie the notion, which is that as people make progress in faith, hope, and love, they develop a sensitivity, an instinct, that enables them to judge what is to be done as a Christian or to think "Christianly" about new problems as they arise.

In that respect, I think it describes something very, very real and very, very important. If any of us thinks back to a spiritual director or someone else without an office to whom we might have gone in facing difficulties and said, "Help me to think through this," we did so because we thought that person had a certain instinct, an ability that we could trust.

Now, if you describe it in that way, it becomes something very, very difficult to quantify. It becomes very difficult to turn into a criterion. How do you determine who these people are who have advanced in faith, hope, and love to the point where their instincts can be trusted? And so, while I believe that there is this reality, I'm not sure that it can be turned into something that becomes a criterion.

It is a bit like when the Second Vatican Council spoke about the bishops of the world, scattered throughout the world, teaching definitively about some matter. It can be extremely difficult to decide when they ever do that, because you hardly ever have a bishop standing up on a Sunday morning and saying, "What now is going to proceed from my mouth is my definitive statement on this matter of faith and morals." That's not the way they do it. They preach or they write a pastoral letter. It becomes very difficult to turn that thing into any kind of criterion. And I think the same thing is true here of the *sensus fidelium*. There is a tendency in this society to think that it can be determined simply by taking a poll. A book came out recently that was the result of a poll, and in the first draft of the introduction it spoke about this draft as the *vox populi vox dei*—the voice of the people, the voice of God. I took vigorous exception to that and it was removed or qualified at least.

If you went back and took polls, as people did in the 1950s, of Catholic attitudes towards racism in the south, to see how people who were going to Mass regularly and had good Mass attendance and so on, viewed racial relations, you would have some difficulty, I hope, in finding the *vox dei* in this. But there is a tendency in that direction.

The supernatural instinct of faith, or this sensitivity that I'm talking about, is described as belonging to believers, and therefore it is not confined. It's an indication that the Spirit is at work directing hearts, illuminating minds in everybody in the church and that therefore, it is a powerful and potential source for knowing the will of God, knowing the truth of God, which the magisterium and anybody else who wants to know this ought—*ought*—to feel obliged to consult.

How it is to be done is another question. That it should be set up in a kind of counter position to the magisterium, I would have a problem with.

PHILIP MURNION: Let me just ask a question—not necessarily to you, Joe—is there any place or any time or occasion where you thought the *sensus fidelium* was well consulted, given the qualifications that you've all introduced and the fact that it is not a poll and, I think the phrase that was used by Avery in his paper was "faithful and mature Catholics" especially should be the ones consulted. Is there any occasion where you thought that was well done?

JAMES CORIDEN: Well, the obvious example that comes to my mind is the consultations before the two pastoral letters of the American bishops, *The Challenge of Peace* and *Economic Justice for All*. From what I knew of those, they were serious hearings of serious Catholic people. I don't know what the process was, but I thought it was quite sophisticated and eminently successful. I thought that was a perfect example of what ought to be done in consulting the faithful.

I think it is difficult to consult the faithful, but it is not impossible. And it isn't best done by polling or market research or something like that, but it isn't arcane either. It's a matter of conversation, of prepared and thoughtful conversation.

JAMES HEFT: It seems to me that one example of the question that you asked, Phil, might be the teaching of Vatican II on marriage where the dual ends of marriage were put together. Where did all that come from, and what was the sensibility that was growing up within members of the church so that the church actually came to a rather significant restatement about the ends of marriage?

I think I am aware of all the cautions that have been mentioned about how difficult it is to quantify the *sensus fidelium*. But I think theology in general in its more academic mode has failed to pay sufficient attention to one source that would be very rich for it. A couple of people have mentioned this source, a greater attention to the lives of the saints. We might want to qualify in a variety of ways and certainly broaden the scope of who could be included in that category—but I do think that a greater sensitivity to holiness, to people's experience of God, should be a very important resource for how we do our thinking about the life of the church.

RICHARD GAILLARDETZ: I'm very interested in what you're saying, Father Dulles, about the *sensus fidelium*. You said that classically the notion of a *sensus fidelium* presupposes a community of faith. These are people converted to the Gospel, and we evaluate their reception of church teaching in that light.

But one of the things I sensed in your paper was a certain asymmetry, because classically when we affirmed the authority of the teaching office of the church, at least if we go back to the early church, it was assumed that the bishops were pastors of local churches. We didn't presuppose an episcopate in which about 35 or 40 percent hold titular sees. We didn't presuppose an episcopate in which more weight was given to those who were not pastors in local churches but rather held positions in a Roman curia. We didn't presuppose the possibility that there might be a real culture gap between a locus of authority in the Vatican and the locus of authority of bishops who are in fact pastors.

I think that's very important. I grant a lot of what has been said here about the *sensus fidelium*, and the fact that you can't just poll people, that you have to take into account whether the believers have experienced a real conversion of heart, and that you have to recognize the possibility that the sense of the people can be compromised by cultural values. However, since the same Spirit that animates the people of God, all the baptized, also assists the bishops by virtue of their episcopal consecration, we have to also grant the possibility that there may be cultural factors that can be impediments to those who hold teaching offices as well. I don't know any way around it—we have to admit the possibility of a kind of clerical culture that can at least be a kind of impediment to effective teaching in the same way that a highly technologized consumer culture can be an impediment to the people of God properly receiving the faith.

If we only focus on how the laity are subject to secular values, and we don't pay attention to the real impediments that can be present for those who exercise the teaching office of the church, we lose credibility. I think we have to address both of those in tandem.

MICHAEL NOVAK: You asked for examples in recent times. The first one I would say is St. Thérèse of Lisieux. In a way, she was outside the official church as much as one could be, although a sister. And I think she had as much impact on the spirituality of the twentieth century as any human being. I think she is an extraordinary figure. I have never been in a Catholic Church anywhere in the world, except once, that doesn't have a picture or a statue of St. Thérèse of Lisieux, and apart from Our Lady or St. Joseph, I don't know of any other saint that is as universally part of Catholic piety today.

The other example I want to pick up again really is extraordinary—the process of doing the pastoral letters. Three features of that process are of tremendous significance.

First of all, some doctoral theses ought to be written on the difference between the first drafts and the third drafts of both pastoral letters because the bishops really listened. It was an extraordinary process. There has never been anything like it in the history of the church. Good faith is shown by the dramatic difference between drafts.

Second, I've often been accused of being in dissent over *The Challenge of Peace*. It was never necessary. Because debate had been called for, we were able to voice our objections early and they were heard. So, when the final document came out, we were able to assent to it.

A third significant point—where we still had disagreements. That also was accounted for within the document, where it said that the closer we get to practical issues—for example, particular weapons systems—the less binding is the authority, and freedom of conscience obtains. The two leading bishops— Archbishop Weakland in the one case and Cardinal Bernardin in the other—conducted a marvelous exercise in which dissent was asked for early, and they heard it sufficiently well. As a result, there wasn't any really serious dissent at the end.

REMBERT WEAKLAND: I have two points I would like to make on the *sensus fidelium*. The first one is, I thoroughly agree you can't do this by polls and that's very important to keep in mind.

I was very impressed when Patriarch Bartholomew spoke at Georgetown (that speech on ecumenism that had everybody upset). He included an interesting passage where he talks about the way in which the faith of the people is expressed in liturgy and how important liturgy is as a locus for faith, so that the *lex credendi* equals the *lex orandi*—the law of believing is the law of praying. I think that also should be very much a part of trying to siphon off, if you will, what is the *sensus fidelium* and how that has stayed among the Orthodox.

And if you hear the Orthodox bishops in Russia talk today on how they sustained the faith for seventy years without any catechesis, without being able to promulgate bibles and so on, they will tell you the only way was through liturgy, by being consistently faithful to their liturgical practice. So, I think that is some aspect of the *sensus fidelium*.

The second part I would like to mention is this: St. Benedict has a very interesting passage about the *pars sanior* in the community. This is a discernment process. The thing I hated most the ten years that I was abbot primate of the Benedictines was having to do canonical visitations. You go into a strange community and you've got to sit there for weeks, listening to everybody. I found the most important thing for me was to find the *pars sanior*. And the *pars sanior* were those who were not selfish but had the community at heart, those who were faithful to the observance. It wasn't long before you began to figure out who are the wisdom figures in this community, who should be listened to. They are not always the most glib, nor the brightest, nor the most theologically trained. And so, the part of discerning the *pars sanior*, I think for a bishop today or anybody in authority, is very important.

Whom do you listen to? If they aren't embedded in the community and they don't have an unselfish kind of holiness with regard to their desire to see the church thrive, then you're suspicious about what they're proposing. So, I think it is more complicated than we think, and it's not done by majority vote all the time.

PHILIP MURNION: Your example is not unlike the example of the pastorals. What's important is the time spent listening and then the voices begin to rise. If I can use an image, the cream begins to rise to the surface gradually. That requires a personal encounter in some way to be discerning.

MARGARET STEINFELS: I don't think anybody thinks we'd ever come to the sense of the faithful by taking polls, but it does seem to me that the sense of the faithful can sometimes be known in a negative way, that is, in a resistance to accepting various claims and teachings.

It goes to the question of trust, and who is deserving of trustworthiness in the church, which was raised in Professor Selznick's paper. You and I know people who dissent on many issues but, for example, they have a wonderful parish pastor. They are never away from the church because they are in the church and at liturgies. They trust their pastor. When Joe talked yesterday about conversion of heart and referred to the Letter of John, it struck me that that kind of Christian impulse, which is so welcoming and so inviting, is resisted by many people because they do not grant that kind of trust. They do not think their pastors, at whatever level, are worthy of the trust that is asked in a passage like that. And so, it's important to have some sense of the negative, resistant quality of the faithful as we think about these things.

GERRY SHEA: I think Archbishop Weakland's comments about his own experience are very telling and I want to say that I think, from my perspective and thinking about people who are in the pews, we're badly in need of bridge mechanisms. Most pastors don't have the time to do the discernment process that leads to that sort of connecting with people. And yet, many people in the church are wanting that connection, feeling far removed from the traditional sense of the faithful. Avery's remarks that people learn about their church from the *USA Today* or a thirty-second report on television and don't get much more is true. We need ways to connect people who are quite understandably very, very occupied with just making ends meet. Everybody in the family is working away, and they are carrying economic burdens that push them into this stressful life. It's very hard to figure out how to overcome this disconnect between the way most people spend their days and experience their relationships. It is one dimension of the secular/sacral problem obviously. I've made some comments like this before. My reflection on a lot of this discussion has been how we have to work at getting people connected in a way that takes the experience of God that people have and tries to bring it out more in the church and make it more part of trying to create this *sensus fidelium*.

ANN LIN: First of all, I want to second everything that Gerry just said. There is a real issue about getting back to the people in the pews, and along those lines I want to say two things. One, as a political scientist I agree that polls are clearly the wrong way to find out the sense of the faithful, but they do allow for one thing that can also be overlooked. Polls can be bad because the answers you get are shaped by the questions you ask, but they can be good because you can get a representative sampling of the people who are out there. The problem with consulting just the people who you discern are the best people to talk to is that, if your discernment process is right, you pick up the dissent as well as the assent; but if your discernment process isn't that good, you tend to listen only to the people who support the sense you came in with of what the problem is. That's a real issue.

The other thing I wanted to say is that one of the places where common ground breaks down is when people who are on the liberal side of the church are accused of not being faithful or pious or devoted enough and, therefore, their opinions don't need to be listened to. And I think one of the sorrows that people on the liberal end of the church carry around is that they do feel very devoted to the church through liturgy and through prayer, but because some of the worship is not in the traditional methods, that piety gets overlooked.

VIRGIL ELIZONDO: I would just like to reemphasize the need, the absolute need, for prayer and ritual. I had the opportunity to participate this year in what I thought was one of the most marvelous events I've ever participated in in Catholicism, the World Youth Day in Paris. The French press had been very negative before the event, had cut it down and had predicted it was going to be a complete failure. That very same press, during and after the event, changed completely. I even read an article recently about how the World Youth Day had marked a major moment in the life of France, a major change, moving it from cynicism to soul and spirit, moving it away from some of their classical philosophers, Voltaire and so forth, to the depth of Catholic ritual.

And I think we sometimes underestimate the real power of our Catholic family and unity. It is far greater than debates and dogmas and doctrines and so forth. We need those, but the deep sense in our Catholic tradition, our treasure, is our ability to celebrate ritual. I think the rituals we've had here are very important. I was not here for the opening ritual, but I heard from several people that it was profound.

So, I think there is something that people know when they are celebrating. In San Antonio we have gotten all kinds of diverse people together, even people who were vehemently anti-Catholic. Not just right or left. We got together on Good Friday because we insisted that Jesus died for all of us and so on Good Friday we can pray together even though we may disagree vehemently on many things.

I personally visited one of the most anti-Catholic ministers in town, who was usually in front of the cathedral with placards talking about the bad things we Catholics do. I went personally to invite him, and he said he'd think about it; and he showed up for the Good Friday service.

There is a profound sense of what I think is the deepest element of our Catholic treasure, our rituals. Rituals allow people the freedom to be very, very different but to be related. The rituals in Paris were beautiful and festive; they were very traditional and yet very modern. I mean, there was dance and there was song and there were people dressed in every way you could think—some very formal with veils on their heads and some almost topless, and everything in between. They're all at the same liturgy, and they're all praying in the same space. I think we need to do more of that. Our society is too divided, and I think Catholicism has that sense of ritual which is, to me, like the *sensus fidelium*. Maybe I am strong because I know that in our Latin American tradition the strongest thing we have is public ritual. That is where we feel connected to each other and to the local church and to the greater church.

So, I would just like to emphasize what Archbishop Weakland said about the Eastern church. I think that has been the experience of the Latin American church. It is ritual that has kept us in the church.

PHILIP SELZNICK: I hesitate to derail this very rich discussion of matters that are from my point of view fairly specialized, but I have a thought that might be of some relevance to the basic issue of the hierarchy and the people. We need a shift in thinking about "the people" from opinion and attitude to condition; our concern has to be for the condition of the people, not just for the opinions or attitudes they express. That requires a rather different form of discernment.

But my basic point is different. It is rather that there is an important sense in which authority resides in a community and that counterposing an officialdom of whatever sort to "the people" misses the point.

For example, if we think of democracy as a sovereignty of the people, or as the consent of the governed, we always have to add qualifications. We have to say, well, not just any consent. It has to be in some sense a self-preserving consent.

When consent is self-preserving, the people are not isolated individuals. They are associated in communities. The people-in-community are bearers of ultimate authority, but that authority is self-limiting. The people have to be acting within a framework that limits what they can choose and even, to some extent, what they can say.

But if the people are limited, so too is the officialdom, and the officialdom cannot embody the community's authority. That lies somewhere else, in the whole community. If that is so, the quality of authority—its nature and efficacy—depends on the quality of community—its cohesion, its divisions, its troubles, its prospects. These are lessons we can glean from political theory. I don't think they are far removed from the special concerns of community in the church.

So the question I raise is: What does it mean to say that authority resides in the community? What will be the consequences of that principle for how we think about the hierarchy and the people?

JOSEPH KOMONCHAK: I think there's a profound sense in which your description of authority as resident in the community is true of the church. The primary bearer of the Gospel from generation to generation is the whole community, and what we call authorities or structures of authority live on the capital of the word in grace that's found in the church. I mean, it's always within the community that there is any kind of authority. In that sense, I'm not saying chronologically, but in that sense, community is prior to authority. Or if you want, authority and community mediate one another. I want to try to indicate that, because there is a tendency to think that it is authority that is generative of community, and I want to argue that there is a sense in which community is generative of authority.

An example is the case of the long, long tradition of considering what the church might do in the case of a heretical pope.

In that is the recognition that you need to belong to the church in order to have even the supreme office of authority in the church. And if you depart from the church in virtue of your ceasing to believe what the church believes, then you cease to have authority in the church. That is extremely crucial. It is a very, very important notion.

PHILIP MURNION: If I can just add to that and bring back the question of worship, the instruction for the Roman missal says: Where is Christ to be found? In the assembly, in the word, in the sacrament, and in the minister—equally. It is the mentioning of the assembly first, in that instruction to the Roman missal, that confirms that.

JOSEPH KOMONCHAK: Right. That's one of the things that got Cardinal Mahony into trouble. I like very much a phrase that Archbishop Weakland used, the wisdom figures. I think that is an extremely important notion. The difficulty often is, of course, that you may have to be wise yourself in order to be able to discern who are the wise. So you get involved in a paradox here, which is another way of indicating the significance of conversation, because it may only be in conversation that these things come out or that your own growth in wisdom may take place.

When I distinguished between the *sensus fidelium* and the results of a poll, it was not in order to put down the polls but to try to indicate that the polls by themselves don't have initial theological valence. I do think that the result of a poll that is well and carefully done may give a precise snapshot of something of the state of the church. I think that is extremely important and has long been neglected, particularly if the snapshot shows some features that people may not wish to acknowledge are present.

Polls therefore become very important. Too many of our conversations about the church take place on the level of prescription—what the church ought to be—with insufficient attention to whether what the church ought to be is what the church is. I think that a poll well done may be extremely important. I mean, I would be willing to bet that if you did a kind of a complete poll, there's nobody in this room who would be completely happy with the results. Whether happy or not you may find yourself having to face this and say, while I find my people are not with me or with the church on questions of race or abortion or the death penalty or whatever, that's where the real value of a poll is. The reason I raise it is that there were some people wanting to move immediately from the results of a poll to theological consequences.

AVERY DULLES: There are so many good points made, I have to be very selective here. In response to Mr. Gaillardetz: There is a real question about the multiplication of auxiliary bishops and curial bishops and so forth. On the other hand, I think it seems to be necessary. It's a development that has taken place with Vatican II, almost a redefinition of the bishop not primarily as the pastor of a local church, although that seems to be usual, but as a member of the *collegium* of those who have supreme responsibility for the direction of the church. And that allows for a number of bishops who have real authority in the church but are concerned with supra-local questions or perhaps within a very large diocese performing functions that are not strictly those of government of the residential bishop.

And I think with the multiplication of interdiocesan committees and bishops' conferences and synods and all the work that is being thrust upon Rome, you do need authority that is not simply confined to the work of the local bishop, who has more than enough to do managing a large diocese. So, I don't think they can devote the attention that needs to be devoted to supra-diocesan questions, which in the modern world really need to be attended to. I therefore doubt that we can really go back to a system where all bishops are heads of local churches and are governing dioceses.

I also think that the clerical culture is a real danger. We talked in our discussion group about people who are seeking promotion in the hierarchy. I don't know what to do, but certainly something has to be done to bring that under control. But I also think that a bishop who is not pastor of a local church can have a very good sense of the Gospel. If he is a prayerful bishop and meditates on the scriptures and so forth, he can be a very responsible Christian leader without necessarily spending a great deal of time attending meetings of pastoral councils and senates or whatever you have of priests nowadays.

That feeds right into what Archbishop Weakland and Virgil Elizondo said about the importance of the liturgy. I couldn't agree more. I think that is the heart of the whole thing and really, we do need, as I think Mr. Shea said, to build up Christian community from the liturgy and to re-create communities of faith where they are lacking so that people can have this as their primary orientation in life.

With regard to what Professor Selznick said, I think it is profoundly true that the members of the hierarchy do not really possess authority in the church. They should be transparent to the authority of Christ, or if you like, to the Holy Spirit; the risen Christ and the Holy Spirit are functionally one, I think.

This is where they have to get their direction. If they don't get it there, then they really don't have authority. They have to be transparent to the direction given from above.

With regard to the presence of Christ, certainly I think that *The Constitution on the Sacred Liturgy*, Article 7, said some very fine things about the multiple presences of Christ, but it should not be neglected that it said he was present *maxime*, most of all, under the eucharistic species. So *that*, rather than the assembly, is the supreme presence of Christ. The assembly does not get transubstantiated. I think that has to be clearly kept in mind, and I hope it wasn't neglected in the pastoral in Los Angeles.

I forgot something I wanted to say about the pastoral letters. I think the process was very good, but I'm not quite sure that it is really the *sensus fidelium* that was at work there. I think it was more people's judgment about economic and military questions, which should certainly be consulted. I don't think that's the type of *sensus fidelium* that Joseph Komonchak was talking about when he talked about the spiritual director, you know, having the *instinctus fidei*—I'm not sure the *instinctus fidei* tells me whether the minimum wage should be lowered or raised.

BRYAN HEHIR: I wanted to go back to the question about examples of what worked. And I will use the pastoral letters as an example, but my primary example, in spite of its outcome, has always been the Birth Control Commission. That is to say, if you looked at how that worked, to some degree it seemed to me exactly what the council called for. It started out as a commission of small specialists. The pope expanded it to include the laity. He expanded it to include scientific disciplines. He then expanded it to include theologians. They had already been on it but they were expanded even further.

My sense of the dynamic of that committee comes from two places. One, I've studied it and taught it for a long time because I have always been fascinated by the dynamic that occurred within it; second, because I had that interest—and John Noonan was there, so he can talk about it—I used to talk to Cardinal Deardon about it all the time. He told me about the meeting of the theologians that he had been asked back to Rome to chair, in which, he said, you had people who had taught this question all their lives. And you would watch some of them walk up to the edge of change, have all the reasons to change, and then ultimately say they couldn't change. And other people who walked up and walked over it.

But my only point is that there was structured discourse there, a rather remarkable example of the church's life. Now, the problem that arises out of it is that—after all of the structured discourse and it obviously was the case—it wasn't definitive by itself. And by constitutional framework the pope could do exactly what he did. But that's an interesting model to look at, different than the pastoral letters and a fascinating one.

The other point I raise about the pastoral letters is the point that Michael made about a differentiated mode of criteria, which I always try to summarize by saying "increasing specificity means declining authority." The interesting thing about that is, that was used for both letters, that's true. But, I don't think you could write a letter at the bishops' conference on bioethical issues and use those criteria. So, the question arises, Are they uniquely applicable to socioeconomic issues or are they valid moral criteria that should be, in principle, applicable to any moral issue in the Catholic tradition? The fact of the matter is, there is no question in my mind that no committee at the bishops' conference could ever have written on bioethical or family or sexual issues and used those criteria. It would be out of the question.

So, then the question is: Have we got an internal contradiction in the theological framework, or have we just got an as yet unparceled out question or, in fact, is it the case that there are some moral issues for which the differentiation of criteria is not acceptable? I think that's an argument that can be looked at.

BENEDICT ASHLEY: Well, I think it is a mistake to put the *sensus fidelium* on one hand and then the magisterium on the other, because in the classical examples it was always the magisterium who consulted the *sensus fidelium,* and that meant that they had to discriminate, as Archbishop Weakland has said, the healthier part of their community in deciding. Look at the Marian doctrines. Those were cases where the pope officially consulted the bishops. Particularly on the Assumption, Pius XII asked the bishops, What do your people believe in your diocese? Would they accept this doctrine?

And I'm sure there were some people who said no. They had to decide then not just by majority but by the kind of people who believed this. Now, that means that in an ideal situation voices would come up from below from all sorts of angles—from the saints, the mystics, the theologians, the ordinary people who witness the Gospel in their lives, and so on. That would come up to the bishop. The bishop would judge about some particular difficulty that is before us. His judgment would go to the pope. He would express his mind to the pope about this, and the pope looking at the whole church would pass his judgment. Because we know well that in history some episcopacies have taken positions that later on turned out to be heretical.

Look at the Arian controversy. There were Arian bishops who would have taken the other position. So, even in the ideal situation this is a process that rises from below to the top. And I think that the only thing that we could do to improve it would be to try to stimulate at the lower level greater contact between the bishops and their people, and to encourage the bishops to speak to the pope or have a council. What else could we do about that?

SCOTT APPLEBY: Father Ben's first line there was a reference to the healthy part of the community, and we've been discussing, following Father Dulles's initial statement, those who account for the *sensus fidelium* or those formed in the spirit of the Gospel. When, beyond that, we want to discern who among them are the voices of wisdom, I think we have to return to a theme that is throughout those lines and that's the question of contemporary formation.

We have to address what is meant by formation and what counts for formed Catholics today. Certainly, we're going to consult the saints and the mystics and the theologians in the process, but I don't know how many of them are immediately apparent to us in the contemporary church. There are some, certainly, but I'm more concerned with a number of issues that fall within this discussion of formation. We've heard a lot about it, and one of the small groups reported "formation, formation, formation" as its major concern. But there are multiple sites of formation in today's church.

There are a whole generation of masters of divinity formed at universities, for example. There is formation that goes on in the parish. There is formation that goes on in the seminary. There is a whole range of things that could be described as some aspects of formation in the university.

It seems that we skirt the question of what counts, in whose minds, for adequate formation that will contribute to an accurate sense of the *sensus fidelium* on these questions. There are a lot of unspoken assumptions about what's going on in the church in terms of forming Catholics, apart from the question of all the many Catholics who we would recognize are not formed at all yet.

And I think not now, but at some future Common Ground discussion perhaps, we ought to be quite explicit about our assumptions about these different levels of formation, different sites of formation. I think one point of disagreement is what voices are to be heard and weighed by different parts of the church, including the leadership, the hierarchy, among this somewhat new and complex culture of Catholic formation with various degrees of contact with the secular world.

PETER CASARELLA: On the question of the *sensus fidelium* we had an extensive discussion of the pluses and minuses of polls, and I certainly agree that we get a better snapshot of the church by either undertaking or responding to polls. I think there also is the deeper question of the kind of "culture of polling" in the church and society. I know as a theologian that it sometimes seems that my job is reduced to responding to the latest poll that says so many Catholics do or don't believe in the Real Presence, or responding to a poll that may talk about some percentage of Hispanics in the church and the way that's going to relate to the Fourth Encuentro coming up in the year 2000.

I find it somewhat problematic, even granting the value of this empirical approach. We are caught up in a culture within church and society that wants to get to the empirical level and then doesn't know, as Joe Komonchak pointed out, how to go from there to the normative question. I think there's an alternative that has been raised by a number of people, and I think that alternative has some consequences for Common Ground—namely, looking at models of holiness in the church, models of holiness that can contribute to the formation of Catholics in the church today.

This is a real way that a number of people have mentioned of getting to the *sensus fidelium*. This is a real way of contributing to a Catholic culture for the third millennium. Michael Novak mentioned the new doctor of the church, St. Thérèse of Lisieux. Some people look to Dorothy Day as a model of holiness. Ana María Díaz-Stevens and I were talking about models of holiness in the Hispanic/Latino tradition, for example, Padre Félix Varela, the nineteenth-century Cuban philosopher and advocate for Irish immigrants in New York City. If common ground is indeed, as we have often stated, "holy ground," then seeking out viable models of holiness is a concrete task we could undertake and, in undertaking that task, contribute to a truly Catholic common ground.

JOSEPH KOMONCHAK: I want to go back to the question that Richard Gaillardetz raised to Father Dulles and to Father Dulles's response, and then link it up with one or two other things that were said. It has to do with the ministry of the bishop. I hope there are no auxiliary bishops here, but my own view is that—no doctrinal qualification follows from this at all, please—simply, I don't see the need for auxiliary bishops. In raising this, Richard named an issue that is exremely important. If you go back and look at *Lumen gentium,* chapter 3 on the hierarchy, with the extensive discussion on the episcopate there, look in the footnotes. Almost all of the footnotes are drawn from Ignatius of Antioch, Cyprian, maybe one from Tertullian, Irenaus, and so on. All of these are drawn from the first two or three centuries of the church's life, when the bishop was the head of a fairly small community, maybe the size of a large parish today, three thousand or four thousand or five thousand people maybe.

Now, if you compare that to the archbishop of New York today, who presides over 1.5 million people and 410 parishes, I begin to raise for myself the question of whether the social difference between the size of the diocese then and now has not reached the point where you have to say that what could be said truly of the role of the bishop in Cyprian's Carthage *cannot* be said of the role of the bishop in the archdiocese of New York.

Hans Küng, when he wrote his book on the church, found only one thing to admire in the church in Italy, and that was the number of dioceses. There were so many of them. Many of them are very, very ancient, and many of them were sort of suburbs, but each of them had a bishop. I would, if you want, multiply the number of bishops. If we're going to continue to say about the bishop what is said in the council and what the tradition said, I would multiply the number of bishops.

Some of you may find this a scary thought, but the reason for saying this is that as long as we don't address that issue and you want to talk about bishops as being persons who are closer to their people than Rome is, and so on, all of those kinds of questions arise, the question of communicating, finding out what your people mean. It's not something that a bishop of an immense diocese can easily do now, but the pastor can do it. So much of what we are asking here of the pastors, of the bishops, is the sort of thing that has to take place by conversation and the building up of communion in far smaller units. I think that's extremely important.

In addition to that, I would raise the issue of whether the role of the bishop has not changed principally to that of an administrator. If you want to see some fierce comments about this, see Louis Bouyer's book *The Church of God*. He has a chapter toward the end about the reduction of the role of the bishop to being simply an administrator to the neglect of what Brian Daley insisted upon the other day, his primary role as a preacher and celebrant of the Eucharist.

You're in danger of turning the whole church into one vast, multinational religious corporation whose main principle of unity and effectiveness is administrative if these sorts of issues are not addressed at some level. There is a sociological tension here between all the things that we want to say and the increased burdens we want to place upon bishops, and their concrete situation vis-à-vis their people, the size of their diocese, and the responsibilities they face or vis-à-vis Rome and Rome's notion of what the role of the bishops should be.

ROBERT IMBELLI: Just a remark with respect to Joe's last point. If indeed bishops are multiplied, and I like that idea, I think one of the gains is precisely the possibility of discerning within a more restricted community and reciprocally the possibility of that more restricted community having a voice in who its pastor will be.

PHILIP MURNION: There is a bishop who wants to have the last word about bishops before we go on to another subject.

OSCAR LIPSCOMB: I don't think you ever get the last word about bishops. Two observations. First of all, most of the titular bishops, I think, are auxiliaries throughout the world. And auxiliary bishops exist precisely to make the bishop closer to the people. All of the vast dioceses are divided into administrative areas in which the auxiliary bishop takes the place of the bishop, at least in being present to the people so they can see a bishop and touch a bishop and feel a bishop's sacramental ministry. Let me tell you, nobody likes to be confirmed without a miter. I suggested that once, and I didn't get very far.

So, they're not all superfluous. They are doing, I think, "bishopy" things, and the first thing a bishop does is not administration, though that might be that for which he is most known. Thirteen times a year I write a letter to the faithful of the Archdiocese of Mobile asking for special collections. That's the thing I'm most known for. But that's not what I do mostly, and that's not where my first energies are.

It is really in preaching and teaching, I think, and sacramental ministry. And I don't know how it works in other groups or provinces but when we gather to talk about candidates for the office of bishop, the first thing we hunt for is a holy person who has a pastoral sensitivity to people. All the rest becomes secondary. I don't know how it is in other places, but there is a concern for these issues. They're not just ignored among the bishops themselves.

MONIKA HELLWIG: I wanted to address a question to Professor Selznick. I thought that his comments subsequent to the exchange of the papers had a perspective that we could have pursued and didn't. Please tell me if I'm not summarizing your position correctly, Professor Selznick. In making the comment that distrust of authority is very limiting of what a society can do, you quietly slid in another comment, that "appeal to the authority of God doesn't settle the practical issues because everyone presumably takes that stance." And then I thought that you had a slant on it that was especially helpful—that the organizational culture of the Catholic Church contains—this was your phrase, "a rich, elaboration of hierarchic structures and perhaps explication of the reasons would help solve the problems."

And I match that with another comment that you made, that careful attention, careful commitment really, to the purposes of institutions was the way to find judgments about whether the claims being made for authority in specific instances were valid in relation to the aims of the community.

PHILIP SELZNICK: That's terrific.

MONIKA HELLWIG: I thought that related very directly to the discussion about authority resting in an extremely broad way, broad in centuries as well as broad in numbers, in the community and its total purpose. It seems to me that that bears a little elaboration from Professor Selznick and comment from the other panel members.

PHILIP SELZNICK: Well, I don't have any quarrel with your summary. I think it captures the point. An elaboration might go on without end, but what I would like to emphasize is that dialogue is inherent in the idea of community, and dialogue is a requisite for effective authority. But dialogue presumes a framework of commitment so that people really listen to one another.

Perhaps I could put it this way. I once wrote that two fundamental elements of community are always in competition. One we can call civility, which is relatively cool and detached. It governs manners and the way we relate to one another, how we listen to one another. The other is piety, which is, you might say, more warm, more committed, engaging virtues of humility and loyalty.

Civility and piety are the great principles of community, and I think every community deals with the connection—and the tension—between civility and piety. The problem is often that we fail to see their connection. If we take a simple example of listening, civility can mean little more than simply taking turns. You wait for somebody to stop talking, and then you talk. And that's reasonably civil; at least you aren't interrupting the other person.

But it is not a genuine civility if you haven't really listened. If you really listen, as the listening deepens, you begin to consider what ideas and feelings you share. In effect you create a community of discourse. The richer that community of discourse, the closer civility comes to piety. Piety is tamed by civility, but the two work in tandem. I say this because it suggests a way of thinking about how the elements of community come together, and how each element must accept a framework of constraint. Civility constrains piety; piety enriches civility and guides it as well.

Father Dulles pointed out that there is indeed a constraint of the Holy Spirit, of God, of Christ, in limiting the authority of the hierarchy. I'm a little unsatisfied because we need to interpret truth in ways that will embrace the whole community. That is to say, to embrace all those who are outside the hierarchy and are, at some level, subject to its authority, but who are also members of a community that is the source of authority. So religious principles, ultimate sources of authority, have to be interpreted and applied with attention to the nature of the community, perhaps especially the ways people experience their connection to the community. And that means, I think, approaching the model we have discussed.

In a sense I feel I have the high office of relating what is going on here to some larger world of ideas and experience. I'm perfectly willing to do that, but I am aware of its limits, and the great danger of being irrelevant. I don't like being irrelevant, but that might be my condition.

Anyway, I do think it is important to pursue these ideas, to meditate on them, and to ask what consequences would follow for understanding authority in a great institution like the Catholic Church.

PHILIP MURNION: Do you want to pick up on that question, Michael? That comment?

MICHAEL NOVAK: Well, it ties in with another point that Professor Selznick made in his paper when he talks about the egalitarian temper of America and the egalitarian temptation to regard hierarchy, on the one hand, and inequality, on the other, as inherently evil. I would like him to elaborate on that a little bit in connection with Alexis de Tocqueville's further criticism about the inevitable tendency of democracies to lead toward conformism. In other words, the powerful impulse to raise up the common man as *the* authoritative voice. Tocqueville goes so far as to say only in an aristocratic society is there true liberty of opinion. If you're rich enough and have enough status, you don't care what other people think of you, and you say what you think.

In a democracy everybody must care what the 25 to 75 band in the middle thinks of them, and there's a tendency to beat down the elites. As you point out, there's a real danger of some of our institutions being overrun because they can only be defended by elites. I want to tie that to a point that Jim Coriden made in his paper on the ethos of the United States. The Catholic sense both of what communion implies and of the high esteem due to the episcopal office diverge from American individualism. But I would also add the American love of "process," which we're exemplifying here. Only in America do people run a meeting the way we are. This is purely American. We are at some point suffocating in process.

PHILIP SELZNICK: Wait a minute. I was in Amsterdam two weeks ago and did the same thing.

MICHAEL NOVAK: Okay, I don't know who learned it from whom, but it certainly does not happen in Italy and in most other places on the continent. The point I'm trying to make is that when we say "American Catholic" we tend to think of all the positive things we have to contribute. We don't say enough about that spirit of conformism, that spirit of consultative "process" that smothers everything in about two feet of peanut butter, and that pulls down everything to a lowest common denominator.

I say that because, especially among a good many conservative Catholics, there is a real worry about the consultative process as process because they are suspicious of the tyranny of what they call process liberalism. It says it is open, but it is not really open. It always ends up in the same product and the same range.

It is very important for us to be alert to that. It comes along with the principle of equality and the principle of liberty. It comes under attractive banners, I'm trying to say, but it ends up in conformism. It is well signaled in that paragraph of Dr. Selznick's.

PHILIP SELZNICK: Thank you, Michael. I would like to tie that point to the suggestion I made earlier that when we think about democracy, and I think that is true of other communities as well, we should be thinking about the people. If we think about the people, we should have to think of the people in community. That is, the people as participating in a structure to which they are committed and which helps answer the question, how is the will of the people governed?

The idea of "people in community" presumes a complex set of institutions, which have some claim to respect. If you have a complex set of institutions, you're also going to have elites.

In my paper I did say something about the egalitarian temptation. This is the temptation to think of all elites as people who are simply holders of privilege or power, without considering the great social functions many elites perform. As Michael suggests, democracy itself depends upon the effective functioning of elites. If the defense of freedom requires eternal vigilance, we need elites to do the work.

The flip side of all of this is that the authority of elites is not self-justifying. If you tie elites to functions, then they must be accountable, that is, assessed in the light of the functions they perform. Consider academic freedom. Academic freedom is not something to be understood as the rights of individual faculty members to go their own way. Academic freedom derives from—and serves—the larger purposes of the institution. The reach and limits of academic freedom are found by looking to the nature of the institution.

Looking to purpose is a very complex matter. Sometimes we have to recognize that fulfilling our purposes—realizing our natures—requires reassessments and reconstruction. In a university context we might decide that academic multiculturalism is too rampant and we ought to find ways of fulfilling the purpose of the institution by encouraging more cross-disciplinary activity. That requires thinking deeply about means and ends.

Somebody once said, I think it was Peter Drucker in talking about American business, that one of the hardest questions for a business leader to answer is "what business are we really in?" That is a profound question, which applies to many other institutions as well.

JAMES CORIDEN: I just wanted to return momentarily to the point that Bryan Hehir made in describing moral methodology and constructing teaching instruments, like pastoral letters, by a process of consultation. What I perceived him to be saying was that in areas of biomedical issues the methodology was unemployable; that it didn't work because of the specificity of the content. And when confronting him with that at the break, he denied it vehemently. Would you make public your denial please, Bryan?

BRYAN HEHIR: Well, my denial is based on the purpose of what I was trying to do. As a constructive statement, my view is that the differentiated methodology, values, principles, rules, and then cases, ought to be applicable across the range of moral issues. In other words, I think you can make a very solid case for it being so.

What I was saying is that if you set up another committee of bishops at the NCCB and said we're going to look at the range of bioethical issues and we're going to use this methodology, they would get a telegram, quickly, that this is not permissible. The bishops may be able to speak more directly to it, but at least it is my conviction that you never could get away with this. The argument would be made that in this other range of issues there is a set of universal principles of a negative nature saying some things never can be done, and therefore you can make those principles concrete in a very specific act and that's the end of it. Therefore, I always thought this argument—that you can go from values to principles to rules to case analysis which would allow, because of empirical complexity, differentiation—was undoable. But I think, in principle, it should be. I was talking about descriptively what would happen.

PHILIP MURNION: Let me hold you right there for a second. You said that when it was applied to bioethical questions it would conclude some things never could be done. The example that was used, minimum wage, was something that ought to be done. Is part of the issue that in some of the other pastorals you're talking about what ought to be done and, in this case, it's a matter of what can't be done?

BRYAN HEHIR: Not necessarily. I mean, there is a complex point here and others can speak to it also. Obviously in the nuclear-war pastoral, we said that direct intentional bombing of civilians is never permissible. Actually, I can remember when Dick McCormick worked through the early phases of the proportionalism argument, it was always a sticking point for him whether he wanted to argue that issue on proportionalist grounds, because he thought you should never do it. So, it does get complicated, but it isn't just between what you're saying what you can do or cannot do.

ANNE E. PATRICK: On this point, it strikes me as relevant that we're discussing a hypothetical medical-ethics consultation and a possible pastoral, but we have that third case of the pastoral that wasn't. The one that never succeeded, which was impeded from the first in terms of the scope of the questions that could be addressed regarding women's concerns, and which met with very dramatic interference in terms of the bishops' conference. So, I think we ought not to forget that example of a pastoral that wasn't, the decade-long effort to compose a pastoral letter on women's concerns that the U.S. bishops abandoned in 1992.

PHILIP MURNION: Avery has spoken to that same subject about the degree of specificity and can criticize, I think, the bishops' conference for getting too specific on some issues and yet would perhaps argue the legitimacy of specificity on some other issues, precisely the kinds of issues that are on the table here. Am I reporting you correctly, Avery?

AVERY DULLES: Well, I think there is a problem raised when they're discussing secular issues—what kind of authority are they speaking with? Some people have felt that the bishops' conferences as such should not put their authority in prudential judgments that are rather far outside the realm of theology and that depend upon rather technical analysis of the economy, or what will result in a secure world without war, and so forth.

They feel it is quite proper for individuals and especially laypeople to be much concerned with these problems, very active in applying Catholic principles to social order. But I think it was Bryan who said the more specific the applications get, the less authority they have, and when they do get down to nitty-gritty details on what kinds of warheads can be manufactured and whether the minimum wage should be raised or lowered, things like that, they raise a great deal of controversy within the Catholic community. Many people who are opposed to the position that the bishops have taken may be just as good Catholics and pious Christians as the ones who agree.

So, that creates a kind of division in the church that is not really on religious grounds, and I think the hierarchy should be cautious in creating that kind of division.

JAMES KELLY: In terms of consultation and common ground and things of that sort, it seems to me that it is precisely these moral issues of sexuality, of gays, of right-to-life issues, that engage the laity on the local level. Bryan's remarks left me thinking, "Well, what's a good alternative?" It seemed as though the *Humanae vitae* discussion failed, and Bryan was skeptical about that being used again.

The extensive dialogic method in terms of the social encyclicals on peace and on economics doesn't seem to be promising either, for the reasons he mentioned. So, in search of good wisdom or in terms of prudential judgment and consultation, what are some of the ways we might begin to think about that both on the local level and in terms of the bishops' conference?

BRYAN HEHIR: Well, I guess I'm having trouble being clear. First of all, I don't know that they wouldn't use the birth-control-commission model again. I think actually it is a very good model. It creates a hard question at the end if you've got a commission of enormous credibility that comes to a conclusion and then the executive still has the right to override the whole thing. But that is what a president of the United States faces every time he sets up a blue-ribbon commission. Whether they'll do it again, I don't know, but it would be a good idea to do it.

The second form of consultation, on the pastorals, I think you could do again too. It may go to Anne Patrick's point. I mean, I see no reason why you couldn't use that model again.

Third, there are two different questions between Avery and myself. One is, and we've debated this before, about whether the bishops prudentially ought to become specific, and I think we're still very divided on that question. We don't agree on it. I think by becoming specific you illustrate the thrust of a principle even though you leave it open for debate. And second, you don't create confusion just over minimum wage; there is hardly less confusion over bioethical issues. But that brings you to the third point that I was trying to raise, which is, take an issue like artificial insemination homologous (artificial insemination within a marriage). If the bishops of the United States said, we think there are overriding principles about sexuality, love, life, and relationships within marriage, but we think on the question of artificial insemination homologous that it is open to diverse conclusions because of specific empirical and normative judgments, I think they would not be allowed to say that.

Now, that's the point. It may be a question of prudence, but it is also a question of moral methodology. In other words, if you can leave open minimum wage and weapon systems that have enormous implications for life and you can't leave open artificial insemination homologous even if you hold all of the other values, why? Is it the moral methodology? Is it the nature of the issues? Are there two different kinds of human issues? Has the church got an insight into one area that it doesn't have into other areas? Is one closer to the faith than the other is? Those are the questions that I think are on the table.

JOSEPH KOMONCHAK: Well, I appreciate very much Bryan's final remark because that was the point I was going to make. Where precisely does the difference lie? I think the last four or five questions he raised precisely point the issue.

I have a question about the basic moral methodology, and I'm perhaps going to be echoing William Murnion[1] here, who took vigorous exception to the distinction between general principles and concrete applications. There is something about this way of doing it—values, general principles, applications—that sounds too deductive to me.

I think that Avery's main point here is a valid one. I mean, if you put in there that the first part is binding, the second part is less binding, the third part is even less binding, I don't find it useful. In the first place, I don't like the use of the term *binding*. It still is that juridical model for teaching, and in the end it is not useful.

The question comes down to that protest—mentioned in my paper—that I received from an undergraduate student when I began a course by saying the U.S. bishops are preparing a pastoral letter on the American economy. "What the hell do bishops know about economics?" was his response. And he wasn't simply asking about a matter of fact, it seems to me, but was really raising an issue.

I think there is a general ecclesial question that can be raised as to whether it is the business of bishops to be doing the second parts of the two pastoral letters, or whether that is not really the province of committed believers knowledgeable about the areas.

PHILIP MURNION: I have a fear that we could have a whole conference devoted to this if we were to pursue it any further. A short remark about it, Michael? I want to let Anne Patrick deliver her last question.

MICHAEL NOVAK: This is to Bryan's point. I'm not prepared to make the argument, but I think I should point out that Pope John Paul II would say that on the life questions that Bryan raised we have not deepened our theology of marriage sufficiently to support where the moral teaching lies. But the moral teaching points in the direction of some revisions in our whole understanding of the covenant relationship of man and woman in marriage as an image of God, which have to be worked into our theology. And that's what the pope has attempted to do. It has not been very well looked at in this country but it is there already achieved. Let me say, it is positive. It hasn't been terribly considered, but Bryan is right on the money. It does require a revisit of the theology to see why it is that you can't use the same methodology in this matter as in social issues. This personal matter is so intimately tied up with our understanding of God and the Trinity, the incarnation as well, that it is of a different order.

ANNE E. PATRICK: This is a general question. And it's about that word *order*. Philip Selznick's paper spoke of the well-ordered system, and Coriden's paper ended up with the agreement that the church requires good order. And as I reflect on the conversation around the table and the points we had of difference, I'm wondering how many of those differences really hinge on a different perception of how much chaos and confusion are appropriate to good order. I wonder whether ideas of order, and the kinds of order that could be considered good, might be explored. I'd be interested in a response from any of our panelists on that.

JOSEPH KOMONCHAK: Well, I think that is a very good question. In talking about the unity of the church I used to use a couple of images. One is a very ancient one of the unity of a choir. I think this is in Ignatius of Antioch, and it is the Holy Spirit, by the way, not the bishop, who is the choir director. It's a lovely image.

Now, you can have various choirs, but if you have a polyphonic choir you've got people doing different things and yet the result is harmonious. Another image might be the West Point Drill Parade, in which all the cadets are doing the same thing in lockstep. A final one would be the New York Knicks championship team in 1969–1970, which was a model of unity, but Willis Reed was not doing what Clyde Frazier was doing. You can start moving in there on images and then try to indicate that there are various ways in which you can have a well-ordered community or society and there is going to be a considerable difference.

But Anne raises an issue that has to do with the negotiation of differences. For me, one of the key things that we have to do is to identify where the differences lie. If we say these are differences in experience is that the end of the story? If they're differences in perspective is that the end of the story? Are all differences simply differences in experience or in perspective?

I should indicate to you that my perspective is that of a New Yorker. For a New Yorker, the discovery of difference is an invitation to argument. If you discover that somebody disagrees with you, a New Yorker's initial reaction is to say, "Well, let me see if I can try and figure out where you went wrong." Or, "What, are you crazy?" You sit down and you begin to talk. There is nothing that is more frustrating to me personally than to hear, "Well, that is your perspective, it's not my perspective."

So, I think maybe we need to spend some time in trying to say how we identify, how we sort out, the differences—and maybe the origins of them, the nature of them and that sort of thing—which is a challenge that lies ahead.

PHILIP MURNION: We need to bring this to an end. The image of a choir—an image of a certain kind of a choir—came to my mind in reading the advice of a bishop of New York to the newly ordained in 1928. He said to them, "If I don't hear a thing about you in the next fifteen years, I'll know you are doing a good job." Fit in.

I do want to again thank the wisdom of this choir. We're not all the same voice to be sure, but everyone has been very helpful and thanks to all of you.

Note

[1] William Murnion, a professor at Ramapo College in New Jersey, wrote an article on the U.S. bishops' pastoral letter on war and peace in which he questioned the distinction the bishops made between general principles and specific applications.—ED.

CATHOLIC COMMON
GROUND INITIATIVE

Cardinal Bernardin Conference
March 6, 7, and 8, 1998

Participants

Dr. R. Scott Appleby
*Cushwa Center, University of
Notre Dame
Notre Dame, IN*

Rev. Benedict M. Ashley, O.P.
*Emeritus, Aquinas Institute
St. Louis, MO*

Rev. James J. Bacik
*Corpus Christi Univ. Parish
Toledo, OH*

Dr. David G. Barker
*The Derwent Consultancy
London, England*

Rev. Jeremiah Boland
*Priests' Placement Board
Archdiocese of Chicago, IL*

Rev. John Boyle
*University of Iowa
Iowa City, IA*

•Dr. Lisa Sowle Cahill
*Boston College
Chestnut Hill, MA*

•Dr. Sidney Callahan
*Author and Lecturer
Irvington, NY*

•Dr. Peter Casarella
*Catholic University of America
Washington, D.C.*

Rev. James A. Coriden
*Washington Theological
Union
Washington, D.C.*

•Rev. Brian Daley, S.J.
*University of Notre Dame
Notre Dame, IN*

•Rev. Cyprian Davis, O.S.B.
*St. Meinrad Seminary
St. Meinrad, IN*

Rev. Jonathan P. DeFelice, O.S.B.
St. Anselm College
Manchester, NH

•Dr. Ana María Díaz-Stevens
Union Theological Seminary
New York, NY

•Mr. Thomas Donnelly
Houston, Donnelly & Meck
Pittsburgh, PA

Most Rev. Thomas G. Doran
Diocese of Rockford, IL

Rev. Msgr. Douglas Doussan
St. Gabriel the Archangel Parish
New Orleans, LA

Rev. Avery Dulles, S.J.
Fordham University
Bronx, NY

•Rev. Virgilio Elizondo
Mexican-American Cultural
Center
San Antonio, TX

Rev. Gerald P. Fogarty, S.J.
University of Virginia
Charlottesville, VA

Dr. Richard R. Gaillardetz
University of St. Thomas, St.
Mary's Seminary Houston, TX

Dr. Maureen Gallagher
Archdiocese of Milwaukee, WI

•Dr. Mary Ann Glendon
Harvard Law School
Cambridge, MA

•Dr. Diana Hayes
Georgetown University
Washington, D.C.

Rev. James L. Heft, S.M.
University of Dayton
Dayton, OH

•Rev. J. Bryan Hehir
Center for International Affairs
Harvard University
Cambridge, MA

Dr. Monika Hellwig
Assn of Catholic Colleges and
Universities
Washington, D.C.

•Rev. Robert Imbelli
Boston College
Chestnut Hill, MA

•Sr. Elizabeth Johnson, C.S.J.
Fordham University
Bronx, NY

•Dr. Cathleen Kaveny
Notre Dame Law School
Notre Dame, IN

Dr. James Kelly
Fordham University
Bronx, NY

Rev. Joseph A. Komonchak
Catholic University of America
Washington, D.C.

Dr. Ann Chih Lin
University of Michigan
Ann Arbor, MI

•**Most Rev. Oscar H. Lipscomb**
Archdiocese of Mobile, AL

•**Cardinal Roger Mahony**
Archdiocese of Los Angeles, CA

Sr. Donna Markham, O.P.
The Southdown Institute
Aurora, Ontario

Sr. Elizabeth McDonough, O.P.
Canon Law Consultant
Henderson, NC

•**Rev. Msgr. Philip J. Murnion**
National Pastoral Life Center
New York, NY

•**Hon. John T. Noonan, Jr.**
U.S. Circuit Court Judge
Berkeley, CA

•**Mr. Michael Novak**
American Enterprise Institute
Washington, D.C.

•**Most Rev. Edward O'Donnell**
Diocese of Lafayette, LA

Sr. Anne E. Patrick, S.N.J.M.
Carleton College
Northfield, MN

•**Most Rev. Daniel E. Pilarczyk**
Archdiocese of Cincinnati, OH

•**Rev. Michael Place**
Catholic Health Association
St. Louis, MO

•**Most Rev. Ricardo Ramirez, C.S.B.**
Diocese of Las Cruces, NM

•**Sr. Katarina Schuth, O.S.F.**
St. Paul Seminary
St. Paul, MN

Rev. Donald Senior, C.P.
Catholic Theological Union
Chicago, IL

Mr. Gerry Shea
AFL-CIO
Washington, D.C.

•**Ms. Margaret O'Brien Steinfels**
Commonweal Magazine
New York, NY

•**Most Rev. Rembert Weakland, O.S.B.**
Archdiocese of Milwaukee, WI

Dr. Philip Selznick—special guest
University of California, Berkeley

• Committee Members

CATHOLIC COMMON GROUND INITIATIVE

Foundational Documents

CARDINAL JOSEPH BERNARDIN AND ARCHBISHOP OSCAR H. LIPSCOMB

Introduction by Monsignor Philip J. Murnion

All the basic documents describing the Catholic Common Ground Initiative gathered together in one volume.

In addition to the original statement "Called to Be Catholic: Church in a Time of Peril," this volume brings together: Cardinal Bernardin's remarks at the August 1996 news conference announcing the initiative; a series of questions and answers in which the Cardinal further explains the endeavor; the Cardinal's October 1996 address "Faithful and Hopeful: The Catholic Common Ground Project"; Archbishop Lipscomb's address at the first Catholic Common Ground Initiative conference in March 1997. In a very useful introduction, Msgr. Philip J. Murnion explains the history and development of the initiative.

0-8245-1716-4; $7.95 paperback

At your bookstore or, to order directly from the publisher, please send check or money order (including $3.00 for the first book and $1.00 for each additional book) to:

THE CROSSROAD PUBLISHING COMPANY
370 LEXINGTON AVENUE, NEW YORK, NY 10017

We hope you enjoyed Church Authority in American Culture.
Thank you for reading it.

herder &
herder